Putting It
Together

Also by Paula McGuire

It Won't Happen to Me: Teenagers Talk About Pregnancy
Coming to North America: From Mexico, Cuba, and Puerto Rico
   (with Susan Garver)

Putting It Together

Teenagers Talk About Family Breakup

Paula McGuire

Foreword by Andrea Marks, M.D.
Director, Adolescent Program
Columbia University
College of Physicians and Surgeons

DELACORTE PRESS/NEW YORK

Published by Delacorte Press
1 Dag Hammarskjold Plaza
New York, New York 10017

Manufactured in the United States of America
First printing

Library of Congress Cataloging in Publication Data

McGuire, Paula.
    Putting it together.

    Includes index.
    Summary: Presents interviews with twenty young people who have experi-
enced family breakup through divorce, separation, or death and with professionals, a child psychiatrist and a psychiatric social worker, who discuss the
general aspects of the problems and feelings brought out by the young people.
    1. Divorce—United States—Juvenile literature.   2. Separation (Psychology)
—Juvenile literature.   3. Children of divorced parents—United States—Atti-
tudes—Juvenile literature.   [1. Divorce.   2. Family problems] I. Title.
HQ834.M37   1987   306.8'8
ISBN 0-385-29564-2
Library of Congress Catalog Card Number: 86-29238

FOR JACK, EDDIE, AND MARY,
WITH LOVE

Contents

Foreword

Andrea Marks, M.D.

The joy, heartache, and challenge of adolescence for all young people is echoed in the conversations in *Putting It Together: Teenagers Talk About Family Breakup.* All adolescents experience the loss of an idealized vision of their parents. The normal process of growing up and establishing a sense of self and independence, of becoming separate and somewhat different from one's parents, involves the realization that Mom and Dad are not perfect, their values not exemplary, and their ability to protect and support not ever-present. The adolescents who experience family breakups through parental divorce, abandonment, or death are faced not only with the loss of an image but also with the unresolvable loss of family structures to which they have become accustomed, and oftentimes with the complete and sudden departure of very important persons from their lives.

The impact of a family breakup is always profound, but the coping ability and coping style of a young person will depend on numerous factors, many of which are demonstrated in the conversations in this book. Perhaps one of the most important is timing. Early adolescents— those approximately eleven to fourteen years old and in junior high school—may have an especially hard time. Their bodies and feelings are changing rapidly; mental abilities that allow for evaluation, reflection, and clarity of feelings and expression are still limited; and the normal developmental task of individuation and separation from parents is only beginning and may become complicated and compromised by a sudden family breakup. It is these very young adolescents who seem the most fearful, confused, sad, and angry. A strongly supportive parent or other adult, a sibling relationship, or a friendship comes in very handy at such a time. Humor, participation in sports, and the ability to rationalize are helpful coping mechanisms.

Early adolescence is a time when feelings related to the loss of a parent many years earlier may first begin to emerge. In addition to the already mentioned task of establishing emotional independence from parents, the early adolescent also begins to develop his or her sexual identity and to think about a future role for himself or herself in society. Both parents play important roles in the process of establishing sexual and societal identities; the absence of one or the other may begin to become sorely felt in early adolescence. A boy who hasn't seen his father since age five may begin to feel this loss most profoundly at age thirteen, especially if he hasn't become close to any other adult male. A girl may also sorely miss a father figure to affirm her blossoming femininity. The loss of one's same-sex parent will have a different effect from the loss of one's opposite-sex parent, but the effect is always significant.

Middle adolescents—those approximately fifteen through eighteen years old and in high school—are particularly vulnerable to peer group–related difficulties in the face of a family breakup. The peer group is normally the prime "authority" for middle adolescents. This is the time when parents normally begin to comment on how infrequently they see their adolescent kids, who seem to prefer to be out with their friends or involved in other non-family-related activities. This normal phenomenon may have unfortunate consequences for the adolescent whose peer activities center around various risk-taking behaviors, including drug and alcohol abuse and unprotected sexual activity. Some adolescents may participate in these health risk behaviors because they have not yet fully begun to realize their own mortality or vulnerability. For others, risk taking may be associated with an underlying depression and subsequent carelessness about their own life, health, or social circumstance. The rate of unnatural or violent deaths among young people from accidents, suicides, and homicides has increased dramatically in recent years. Accidents are the leading cause of death among young people, followed by homicide and suicide.

Sometimes role reversal or blurring of role differentiation seems to occur between an adolescent and a parent. The overwhelmed parent may actually be cared for by the adolescent, or may allow the adolescent to be inadequately supervised and to set his or her own limits. Many of the young people in this book are craving more discipline, rootedness, and structure in their lives. Some have had to leave home in order to find this.

Finally, it is important to discuss in a bit more detail the issue of depression. Depression, as an emotional state of children and adolescents, has not been as well studied or understood as depression in adults. Some degree of depression—oftentimes profound—always accompanies family breakup and will occur in all family members.

The depressed person is *sad* about the loss of a family member, *guilty* about repressed hostility, and *ashamed* of feeling unworthy or unloved.

The characteristic signs of depression in adults, such as sluggishness, sleeping difficulty, and poor appetite, may not be apparent in the depressed adolescent. If parents, siblings, friends, teachers, and physicians are to recognize that an adolescent is depressed, and offer that adolescent the help he or she needs, then they must be alert to certain more subtle or seemingly atypical signs of depression. A depressed adolescent may withdraw and become apathetic, or alternatively may behave in a garrulous or aggressive manner. The young person may become sullen and unkempt, limit his or her friendships, become excessively involved in schoolwork, or perhaps experience a decrease in school performance. Sleeping and eating disorders may occur, and various bodily concerns may bring the adolescent to a physician's attention. Chronic complaints of headache, dizziness, or pains in the chest, abdomen, or limbs may in fact be signs of depression. Depression may be manifested by tantrums or incorrigibility, truancy and school failure, running away, delinquency, drug and alcohol abuse, sexual promiscuity, or frequent accidents.

The brave voices of the young people in this book must be heard clearly. Their stories are an inspiration in some cases and a challenge in others; in all cases they provide a message to all who may be in a position to reach out to them—and to learn from their experience.

Introduction

A few years ago Delacorte editor Olga Litowinsky suggested that I put together a book of interviews for young people about adolescent pregnancy. I jumped at the chance. As mother of a preteenaged daughter, I wanted to know more about a problem that was becoming a national disaster. What I learned from fifteen wonderful young women appears in *It Won't Happen to Me: Teenagers Talk About Pregnancy* (New York: Delacorte Press, 1982).

Nearly half of the young women I interviewed had also experienced a family breakup through parental divorce, abandonment, or death. Furthermore, some of the young women were in effect creating broken families themselves, either by not marrying the fathers of their own children or by giving up their children for adoption. Family breakup was a subject that also hit close to home for me because I had married a divorced man with two teenaged sons long before my own daughter was born. As a new wife and, heaven knows, an inexperienced parent, I had lots to learn about teenagers and the effects of family breakup.

Life was often not easy for any of us, but surely hardest for the boys. I became acutely aware of the many difficulties, mistakes, and heartaches that simply don't seem to be avoidable for parents and kids in dealing with a family breakup. One aid I looked for—both years ago and more recently—was material written directly for adolescents, but I found very little. I decided to explore the subject myself in interviews with teenagers so that they could describe how it feels to experience a family breakup. I broadened the idea of breakup to include not only parental divorce or death, but also temporary parental separation, teenagers living apart from their families, and in one extreme case, the homicide of a parent. My editor was enthusiastic, and this book is the result.

The purpose of this book is not to provide new explanations but simply to publish the acutely felt first-person accounts of teenagers in the hope that they might be a source of help or understanding for other teenagers. Most of the circumstances faced by the young people I interviewed were not of their own making, and having listened to them struggle with their words and emotions, I came away with respect for their strengths and vulnerabilities and with profound admiration for the courage and determination so often displayed in the face of enormous problems.

I came to realize that parents, understandably overwhelmed by the problems themselves, can sometimes lose touch with the very kids they are desperately trying to help, thus causing worse problems than before.

Even professionals, social workers and therapists of all kinds, are not perfect: they are often overworked or for one reason or another simply unable to develop a beneficial relationship with a young person who needs help—

something I learned from my own family's experience, as well as from the kids and the professionals I interviewed. So while these interviews are primarily intended to reach out to teenagers, I also hope that the moving voices of these young people will make themselves heard in the hearts of other parents and the many caring professionals who work with kids.

I would like to thank those eighteen young people who are interviewed here. Their names, families, hometowns, and other identifying circumstances have been changed or disguised to protect their privacy.

I also owe thanks to the four professionals who are interviewed in the book. Their knowledge and experience help us better understand the lives of adolescents and often clarify some of the problems and reactions that my group of teenagers had. The identities of these professional people have been disguised in order to further protect those young people in the book whom they knew and worked with.

Other advisers helped immeasurably in the planning and research for the book. They include Budd Robertson, Andrée Marks, Mary Inzana, Nancy White, Sharon Powell, Toni Flint, Jim Stabile, and Linda Loberg, and they have my sincere thanks.

Olga Litowinsky gave invaluable editorial guidance, and Dick Lidz and Susan Gordon read the manuscript and provided able advice. Cindy Feldner made sure the final version was not only accurate but beautiful on her new word processor.

PAULA McGUIRE
Princeton, August 1985

Putting It
Together

Sarah

Reaching Out Can Make
All the Difference

Sarah is a psychiatric social worker in a family counseling agency located in a large midwestern city. The agency specializes in marital counseling and child guidance. Parents and their children may be counseled together or separately. Problems arising through divorce are the major concern of the staff, which includes psychiatrists, psychologists, social workers, and child development specialists.

Many of the young people we see have problems stemming from separations and divorces. Often the parents are still fighting, and the needs of the kids are not being considered. There is much bitterness and recrimination. Most people are not prepared for divorce and are not trained to cope with the sudden changes divorce brings about. Occasionally there has been a prolonged separation without any divorce, or there has been a divorce but the family members are having difficulty moving on with their lives. They are trying to resolve feelings about the family breakup and may still have hopes of reunion. The parents are the ones we ultimately focus on, but we also work with the kids, because it is an important way of helping the family.

Divorce and separation create a crisis and a threat to basic needs. They raise anxiety and fear in kids, no matter what the age. They also challenge people to find new ways of solving problems in the family, and the kids and parents can grow from the experience. But initially divorce is experienced as a threat and a loss.

Children confronted by parents' divorce go through nearly the same mourning process as those who have suffered bereavement. This process is marked by stages, which may overlap and may not follow strictly the order in which they are here described. At first a child may deny that there is a problem or may cling to the belief that everything is all right. I've heard kids say, "Oh, I know they're not really going to get a divorce. They're going to stay married. This isn't really happening." This is the denial stage.

Next the child may experience great sadness over the loss of a parent and the disruption of family life. This is the depression stage. Sometimes the parent who leaves may be one the child didn't know well or wasn't close to. Maybe it was a father who traveled a lot. But the departure represents the loss of what "family" meant to the child, including the goals, the dreams, and the shared values. The depth and duration of the depression stage depends upon how many other changes have occurred during or after the divorce. Perhaps moving and going to a new school, having to make new friends. Perhaps not having as much money.

The depression stage may precede, follow, or alternate with the anger stage. Children of divorce often feel hurt and angry toward both parents. However, it is not uncommon for the custodial parent to say that the children express anger toward him or her rather than toward the parent who isn't there anymore. Kids may feel it's safer to get angry with a parent who has proved to be available.

Of course some kids express a good deal of anger toward the parent who is away. It depends on the family. Sometimes a child feels free to express only negative feeling about the parent who left because any show of positive feelings might jeopardize the relationship with a fragile custodial parent. An extremely anxious and upset custodial parent needs a child to accept his or her own negative view of how the other parent behaves.

Kids who are overly close to one parent or the other have the hardest time, because they experience the divorce as if it was happening to them too. Kids who are dependent on their mothers, for example, feel more protective of them and more angry with their fathers than kids who have been able to lead their own lives. Much of course depends also on the age of the children.

Kids move toward readjustment and acceptance when they see that their parents are beginning to deal with each other more maturely, with less fighting, and with less involvement of their kids as allies. Then the children begin to adapt to change.

Acceptance is the final step in the mourning process. But whereas death is final, an unresolved divorce sometimes holds out hope for a reconciliation, and this can make the path toward adjustment more difficult. Children's final acceptance of a divorce comes when they are able to maintain a satisfying relationship with each parent despite the family breakup.

Children are egocentric. It is natural for them to focus

on themselves when there's a threat, to worry about what's going to happen to them, and to see themselves as the only ones affected by any situation. A child has a hard time understanding that a divorce is not the end of the world, especially if the parents are feeling shaky themselves and are unable to be helpful.

Studies have been written about the effect of divorce on children of different ages.* Divorce may affect the preschool child between the ages of three and five in a number of ways. There may be an acute reaction in toilet training and eating habits. There may be increased irritability, whining, crying, and general fearfulness. Children may be afraid to go to school or afraid to go to bed at night. They may show regressive behavior, such as thumb sucking and blanket holding. They may act out in temper tantrums. On the other hand, they might become preoccupied with being little adults and be cooperative. Both extremes can occur.

Kids who are four and five—an extremely sensitive age—often blame themselves for the divorce. Johnny may express through his play that he was bad and so Mommy and Daddy got a divorce.

Kids of five and six may have a more favorable adjustment if they're already involved in school, enjoying it, and having a life outside of the home and separate from the parents. On the other hand, kids who are having a negative reaction to a divorce may also be having a difficult time in school. They may also have fantasies about the parents returning to each other.

In kids around seven and eight, more sadness and grieving is apparent. At this age they have developed to the point where they are beginning to be aware of a

---

* See especially Judith S. Wallerstein and Joan Berlin Kelly, *Surviving the Breakup: How Children and Parents Cope With Divorce* (New York: Basic Books, 1980).

personal self, an "I," who has feelings of sadness and pain. They're also more aware of their dependency on their parents. They, too, may have very strong reconciliation fantasies.

There is a lot of anger at this age, too, complicated by the fear of expressing it to the parent who left the home. Johnny might verbalize his anger *about* that parent, but it may be very hard for him actually to say *to* that parent, "Boy, you really make me mad!" He's afraid of antagonizing that parent for fear of driving him or her further away. I've also seen children behave badly, almost as if they were trying to distract a depressed parent at home from the parent's own grief. It is as if by giving that parent something else to worry about, they are saving the parent from having to experience the loss and pain of divorce.

Children of this age are subject to conflicts of loyalty; they feel they have to reject one parent and ally with the other. That's probably one of the hardest things to deal with. As kids get older and achieve more emotional distance, they can talk about a conflict and try to resolve it. But if a seven- or eight-year-old chooses one parent over the other, it's going to be hard to shake this choice and later on reach out to the neglected parent.

Kids around the ages of nine and ten often feel ashamed of themselves and their parents. They see themselves as unlovable, and they hold themselves off from sharing themselves with friends. They get all bottled up. And that's probably when they really *need* to share with others. Ultimately they need to talk things out with their parents, but in the meantime, if they could talk with a friend or a concerned adult, kids might find help.

There is also a fear of being abandoned—"Who's going to take care of me?" Very often parents are pretty much out of commission and can't provide much support. The parent taking care of the child may be functioning so poorly that the child may have to take care of the parent.

Divorce is painful for adolescents too. A girl I'm working with now is caught in a loyalty conflict. She feels guilty about even wanting to see her father. She often takes a detached stance: "I don't know what's going on. It doesn't really affect me." But I sense that beneath that stance is a lot of emotional turmoil—anger and sadness and feelings of embarrassment. Adolescents can have a difficult time talking to friends about divorce, especially friends who haven't gone through the experience. They may feel like failures coming from "broken homes." And they may be anxious about marriage for themselves in the future.

Very often adolescents simply can't express themselves at first. They can be unresponsive or full of bravado—you're not sure what the message is. You find out more from their behavior than from their words.

One thing divorce often does is to force the adolescent to look at each parent as an individual, an individual who has both strengths and weaknesses. Some teenagers have a remarkable ability to assess their parents realistically and also be compassionate. Going through a family breakup often enables a teenager to give up illusions about his or her parents and accept them as people who have problems and not all the answers. They are no longer idols: they are human.

On the other hand, teenagers are feeling vulnerable, too, and it is frightening to have feelings of helplessness and to know you can't control what is happening. Some adolescents will withdraw and try to get more involved in activities outside the house. Others will do just the opposite. I know one set of young people aged twenty-one, nineteen, fifteen, and thirteen who have all stayed at home with the divorced mother, doing very little outside the house, just clustering around her and trying to bolster her up.

Self-destructive acting-out behavior—such as drug abuse, drinking, and stealing—is sometimes associated with divorce. Curbing that behavior really depends on how the parents are functioning and how effectively they can negotiate with their adolescent offspring. If the self-destructive behavior has shown itself before the divorce, the family breakup crisis may aggravate it.

I don't know which age group handles itself best when a divorce occurs. It's hard to say, but if there is one child in the family—no matter what the age—who has become close with one parent and permanently alienated from the other, that child usually suffers. Generally speaking, if an adolescent has progressed normally through childhood, has done well in school, has friends, and is not tied into an alliance with one parent or the other, he or she is going to be able to handle the divorce better than a younger child.

I know of a fourteen-year-old girl who has *not* been able to extricate herself from her mother's problems. She was a save-the-marriage baby,* the youngest child. The parents separated when she was five, and from that time on she was with her mother. The mother had a difficult time. The child would fail in her schoolwork and wouldn't want to go to school. She had stomachaches and headaches. She was compliant in the home—never upset her mother, hated conflict, would run to her room when anybody fought.

After nine years of separation the father finally decided to file for divorce, which threw the mother into a complete tailspin. The girl started to drink—setting it up

---

* A child purposely conceived by a quarreling or estranged couple in the hope of giving new life to their troubled marriage.

so that the mother would find out. The mother had never been to counseling and didn't like asking for help. I don't think she would have gone for help ordinarily, but the child had the problem, and it scared the heck out of the mother. So I've been working with the mother and the daughter, and occasionally I've had to bring in the father. But the mother has been emotionally upset while going through the divorce. She has really been blaming the father for everything and now has tried to keep him from coming in. She says she does not even want to talk to him.

The ideal thing is for children to hear the decision about divorce from both parents and have both parents talk to them. The child needs to know that the divorce was not his or her fault. But this didn't happen in this case, and I think that's why the girl is having a problem. She has a real sense of failure. I don't think she ever knew she was a save-the-marriage baby, but on some level kids know if they serve an important role in their family.

This girl is pretty stuck. Along the way she's had many developmental lags and has to make up for them now. For example, she's been so tied up with her mother and the family problems that she has not been able to make friends. So our job is to try to get the mother to become more active and to try to get her to base her identity more on doing something for herself than on bad-mouthing her ex-husband. Then the daughter may begin to lead more of her own life instead of functioning as her mother's total support system.

There's such a thing as emotional divorce without an actual legal divorce. People stay together, continue to live in the same place and remain legally married, but have little emotional connection with each other. Although divorce may never be the best solution to a problem, sometimes people can use divorce to learn from. So long as people understand that their problems are not exclusively rooted in their partners and that they cannot get rid of their problems by getting rid of their partners, they can learn about their own part in bringing about the end of the marriage. And this can be a constructive experience for both parents and children. But people rarely do this! In fact, you wonder what it is going to teach kids about handling problems later on with their own spouses. Are they going to see divorce as the only way out? Sometimes divorce is the best solution; other times people can work out their problems and stay together.

Divorce can have real benefits. For instance, the father on his own can get closer to his kids than he ever was in the marriage. One father described what happened after he got divorced from his wife. For the first time in his life he felt panicky in the middle of the night, and he crawled into bed with his thirteen-year-old son and just clung to him. This was the first time he had ever been able to acknowledge that he wasn't just an important business executive, that he was also somebody who needed nurturing and caring. He never *had* to acknowledge it before. It really helped the kid to see his father as a real person with weaknesses as well as competencies. I'm sure there are often positive results that come of divorce, but we mainly see the people who are stuck!

Death and divorce both need to be recognized as part of one's life—it's something that happens. It's what the family does with it that makes the difference. It's important that families deal with the kids directly about it, have both parents touch base with the children if at all possible. (The sudden death of a parent poses a somewhat different problem.) Assuring the kids they're in no way responsible for either the death or the divorce and that they will still have the support of both parents or the surviving parent; recognizing that it's a difficult time; keeping the communications open; and not trying to shield or overprotect the kids are all important guidelines for parents at these times of crisis.

Since the sixties and the Vietnam War and the eruption of the youth movement with its loss of faith in those in authority, teenagers have been too often left to their own devices and without much guidance for solving their problems. There's no blueprint for behavior anymore, and I think that makes young people more vulnerable. It's a much more confusing time now, when kids are exposed to a variety of life-styles and can get caught up in easy solutions—drugs, alcohol, and fast relationships. Divorce is just part of this whole shake-up, and often the adults undergoing a divorce find it a challenge just to hold *themselves* together, much less to offer guidance and nurturance to struggling adolescents.

There is a real need for stronger parental and institutional guidance. You certainly don't get much support from the federal government or other institutions for helping kids. It shows in the scarcity of day-care facilities, the reluctance of industry to provide job-sharing arrangements with flexible time for parents, the difficulty in obtaining paternity leaves for fathers—it's just part of the whole society. I don't think we are organized to meet the needs of kids right now. The kids have gotten lost in the shuffle.

As a result, kids often feel pretty much alone in dealing with such problems as family breakup. I always urge a kid in this fix to find a friend to talk to. Not feeling so alone is probably the first step. Kids really need each other at such a time. It may also be helpful to find a caring but objective adult—an aunt, an uncle, a friend's parent—who may provide a natural, ongoing support for the young person. That might even be better than formal counseling with an agency or a private counselor. Reaching out to *somebody* can make all the difference.

Michael

Trying to Put It All Together Again

Michael is thirteen and looks younger. He is nervous and inarticulate but tries to appear under control. He is sad and desperately worried about his mother, as his story of her mental breakdown and attempted suicide reveals. He has also had to contend with his sister's lack of understanding, his father's remarriage, a move to a new home in the suburbs, and a change of schools. It may take a while to "put it all together again" as he wants it.

My mother and father split up when I was three. I'm thirteen now. My mother was pretty upset. Also, around that time my father's mother died, and he was all mixed up and didn't know what to do. I felt like that too. Anyway, they got divorced.

I lived with my mother for several years. She got a secretarial job, but after a while she didn't want to go to work. She missed my father. She tried to get over it, but she wanted him back. She was very upset, became a little bit insane, crazy. Finally she tried to kill herself. That was a few months ago. One day I came home from school —I was with my sister—and she was lying on the floor. We knew it was an overdose of pills. Aspirin. So I called the ambulance. Then the police came. We couldn't reach my father at first, but finally he came and picked us up. Since then we've lived with him.

She didn't die then, she was all right. But it's hard now because I don't know what's going to happen to my mother. She's living with her father now. She's still a little bit crazy. We hope she'll try to straighten herself out. But it's hard, because we're always afraid of what might happen.

My father got married again about two or three years ago, so this is all very new for my sister and me. It seems to be working out. I like the new school. I'm making friends. My sister is doing pretty well too. She's eleven. I'm interested in sports: basketball, football, hockey. Whatever I get a chance to do, I do. I have to work at my homework too. When I was in the old school in the city, I didn't do too well. There were a lot of interruptions. With my mom I was always worrying about what was going to happen next. Now I'm getting A's and B's.

So my parents are really happy that I'm doing well. And my stepmother is doing well. She provides like a mother, and my father's happier than he was before. He got custody and is happy that we're safe.

When my parents split up, I was too little to know what was happening. I was about six before I realized what was going on. At first I thought it was my father's fault, then I thought it was my mother's fault, but it was not really anybody's fault. I tried to help my mother through it, but when she really began to go crazy, it was a pretty upsetting time. I visited my father every other weekend then, and he was the only one I could talk to about it. Except maybe my dog. I used to talk to him a lot. But there weren't any friends or anyone else I could talk to.

My main feelings now are of concern for my mother. Sometimes I'm a little worried and sometimes I'm a lot worried. But all the time I'm worried! I haven't seen her again yet. I'm supposed to see her next weekend, but we're trying to find out what might happen, because it will be so upsetting for her. My mother isn't really a person to talk to now. When she gets better, I'll see her again. Otherwise I'm quite happy to be in this house.

My mother thinks I left only because of that overdose of aspirin. But that's not the only reason. I think she should have straightened herself out by herself. Life is life. It was kind of hard on me and my sister to be with her, especially when she began to go crazy.

My sister and I discuss all this—about my mother and the divorce—sometimes. We talk about the bad times, about why she doesn't try to pull herself together. Let's hope she does try. My sister is a little more critical of my mother than I am because she really doesn't like her so much. She doesn't like the way my mother couldn't take life the way she should have. I understand sometimes that some people *can't* take life the way others can. So I think I have a little more understanding for her than my sister does. On the other hand, the way she took life is not the right way either.

I feel better now that things are sorted out a little. In fact, I'm feeling pretty good today. I'm getting my bike, I just had my confirmation yesterday, and my birthday is coming up soon. I am happier than I was before.

I feel sometimes—when I go to church or talk to a

priest—I feel in my heart a little bad for my mother, because people like that, they can't take care of life. Those kinds of people really need help. Mental help. But she doesn't want it. She keeps bothering people, and trying to hurt people, like when she was crazy. She still is, I guess. She did a lot of bad things. She really wasn't like a mother. My sister and I used to have to clean the whole house and do all the cooking. We tried to help her, but she wouldn't listen to us. We tried, everybody tried.

It's always the same feeling of worry, but I think I can get through this. You know, people can get through or they can't get through, or they're a little bit half and half. I'm half and half. I guess I really don't know if I can get through it or not. It might be good to have some support. I know lots of kids in this situation get help from some-body—a counselor, or at school, or a priest or a minister. My stepmother and my father, they help a lot.

My sister worries sometimes, but she doesn't worry like I do. When we used to call my mother, my sister said to her, "I don't love you. I think you should do something for yourself." I urged my mother to start picking herself up too. You can't push life around. I said, "Stop worrying about the past. Think about the future and what's going to happen next."

She would never listen to anybody. She just went into herself and the emotions that happened in the past. She's not getting help from anybody, and a person really ought to try to get help. Maybe if she tried, my father might help her a little. Not too much, but just enough to give her a push. But she's not even trying, and she owes it to herself.

We try to forget the whole business about my mother now. We don't really like to bring it up. We're trying to keep it out of our minds. If something really bad happens, then we'll help. But now we're just trying to get back together and pick ourselves up. It's a bad thing that happened, and there are a lot of emotions around. People got hurt and are trying to put it all together again.

Quentin and Peter

Don't Take Sides

Quentin is fourteen and in the ninth grade in a suburban high school. His brother Peter is twelve and in the seventh grade in the local junior high school. Their mother left the family some years ago and their father later remarried. These talkative boys come on like a vaudeville act, handing each other cues and fast lines, then exploding into laughter at their own jokes. Their high spirits are infectious, and it is easy to see how they have supported each other through teamwork and mutual affection. A devoted father and stepmother also helped.

QUENTIN: It all started when we were living abroad in South America, where my father had a job. My earliest memory of what happened was my mom looking real tired one morning. I went in and said, "Mom, you look like you need a vacation." A couple of days later she said she was going away for three weeks to have a rest. When the three weeks were up, I went to where she was living and visited her. She stayed there. I was about nine, and I realized something was wrong, but I don't really remember when they told us that they were actually getting a divorce. For a little while I blamed myself for their splitting up because I told her she needed a vacation. And then I thought that was pretty dumb.

PETER: I remember my mother had an apartment about ten miles away in this beach area, a really nice place. There was an abandoned monastery nearby where we used to play. Somehow we found out—I don't remember how—but we realized after a pretty long while that she wasn't going to come back home. I wasn't really heartbroken. I felt okay about it because I knew it would be best for my mom and dad. I remember when I was about four or five, I had a nightmare one night. I went and knocked on their bedroom door, and they were having a violent argument. I remember my dad said, "Sorry, Peter, we're having a little argument." And my mother screamed out, "No, we're having a fight!" I was terrified that they were hurting each other. So I felt better that they were away from each other.

QUENTIN: I never knew that they fought. It was all a big surprise to me. Later they told me stuff about how it was never a really great marriage, but it surprised me. I didn't think they were having problems. I took it as if it were a new change—that was what was going to happen, and I couldn't control it.

PETER: I thought, "Oh, no! They're having a divorce!" I felt surprised, but looking back, I realized that their marriage really wasn't good since I could remember.

QUENTIN: I can remember going on a trip with this guy our mother was living with, who was a lot younger than she was. We were going to buy a farm way out from where we were living. My mother has a way of making things sound terrific. To a nine-year-old it was the land-of-milk-and-honey kind of thing.

PETER: We were going to get a hundred-acre farm, and it was going to be really good.

QUENTIN: We came back, and both parents sat us down in the living room. "Okay," they said, "where do you want to live? You can live with Dad or on the farm with Mom."

PETER: I didn't decide. I left it to Quentin. Because I was too young to make decisions like that. I wanted to be with Quentin.

QUENTIN: I never trusted Mom much. She was never very reliable. And now that I was older and kind of looking at things from a real-world point of view, I realized I didn't trust her. So I decided I wanted to live with Dad, and Peter just went along with me.

So then we got into all these guilt trips about my mom. It was all very confusing. She made us feel guilty. She said we abandoned her by deciding to live with our father.

PETER: I didn't know why I felt guilty. I just went with Quentin. I didn't know what side to take. I felt quite alone. And the only thing I could hold onto was Quentin, so I decided to do whatever Quentin did. And that happened for a long time. Whenever Quentin and my dad or mom would have an argument, I'd always take Quentin's side, because I thought Quentin knew what was best for me.

QUENTIN: So as a result of that, I took the brunt of every guilt trip that my mother laid on me. I still don't understand what she meant by a lot of it. She used to say I abandoned her.

PETER: And that it was her sacrifice that she was leaving us with our father. She said to a friend once that children always leave their parents—she just left her children early. I was bewildered at that.

QUENTIN: It was really a justification for not being able to handle us. I don't think she could take on the responsibility of having two kids. I don't think she could handle that and have the same kind of life-style she has now, which she enjoys a lot. More power to her! I don't have any bad feelings toward her. I like her a lot. But I still wouldn't want to live with her. I wouldn't trust her.

❧ PETER: She said she was doing all this for us. I remember she said once that she was leaving us with our father because she knew our father could handle us better. But that it was a great sacrifice for her and was very upsetting for her.

QUENTIN: Then I believed everything she said. Now I've sat back and looked at it from a more adult perspective. I'm a little bit more independent than I was then, and I can look back at what happened and think about it in a more clear way. I think she knew that it was best for us to live with Dad. I think that it did cause her a lot of pain. But I think that what she was doing was bending the truth so that she wouldn't feel so bad about not even trying to take on the responsibility of raising us.

PETER: Once she was telling us vividly about all these major sacrifices that she was making in our best interest, and I couldn't understand what she was talking about. For about a year and a half, two years, we lived with our father, and once a week our mother would take us out and we'd do fun things. This was still in South America. I remember thinking of my mother as a kind of playmate, someone to play with.

QUENTIN: They weren't divorced yet then, they were just legally separated.

PETER: I remember thinking it was fun to be with my mom because we'd always go out for matzo ball soup, and I really liked that. And then we'd go to the beach and play on this contraption that I really liked. I thought of her as so much fun to be with. But I've come to think of my father and stepmother as being my *parents*.

QUENTIN: So basically I guess you could say we rolled with the punches. It never really knocked me for a loop. I don't know, now it's kind of funny, some of it. It's all kind of weird, but none of it hit me like an atomic bomb.

PETER: Me either. I could always talk to Quentin about it.

QUENTIN: Peter talked to me, and I talked to Dad. We were able to work it through.

PETER: I read this book called *It's Not the End of the World*, by Judy Blume,* and this girl is screaming and crying in a restaurant. That was stupid, I thought.

QUENTIN: And the stuff on television was really bad.

PETER: Kids read that and think, "Oh, no, divorce is going to be so horrible and heartbreaking. It's going to shatter me all at once. I'm not going to have any friends, and I'm not going to be popular at school." It wasn't like that. To me it was like a little bit sad, a little bit sad, a little bit sad. You take it piece by piece, a little at a time.

QUENTIN: I know lots of kids who have been through a divorce. I can think of only one kid that I know who lives in the stereotypical family—father, mother, sisters and brothers—perfect home. No divorces or any problems like that. So that most of the people I know take it very calmly. It *is* a pretty big influence on their lives, but it's not like going blind or something! What I've begun to realize is that I'd be a different person if I'd lived with my mother. So the way I think now is different, and the way I handle situations. My experience is different than

---

* Scarsdale, N.Y.: Bradbury Press, 1972; New York: Dell, 1986.

if they hadn't been divorced and continued to live together in a really terrible marriage.

PETER: I used to have a friend in school whose parents were divorced. I used to exchange experiences with him and we'd handle problems together. It was great, because he was my age, and I could relate to him. We looked at things the same way. We used to take our aggressions out on the third graders and stuff like that.

QUENTIN: When the divorce came about, everything went pretty fast. In a strange, twisted way, they showed us the agreement, quickly read it to us—whooosh! "Get it? Right. And you get to see Mom, et cetera, et cetera." Bam! It was such a problem at the time, because Mom, my stepmother—she was living with us then, we knew they were going to get married—was getting a Ph.D. at the time, and that was a big strain. She was going through the final steps of her thesis, the deadlines, the copying, the binding and all. And there were the actual divorce procedures, courts and the bargaining and all that stuff. It was a pain. It was really a pain. It put everybody in a bad mood.

PETER: There'd be arguments about simple stuff. "Peter, you left your book on the table!" I hate that!

QUENTIN: And Peter would kind of step in the wrong direction and whooosh, he'd get set down hard!

PETER: And for a while after the divorce, about a year, I felt confused. I felt guilty that I didn't feel as upset as I should. Then I realized after a while that all the things I read were probably lies. From experience I knew that they weren't really true. There was one book that I read that I thought was really good, called *The Boys and Girls Book About Divorce*. It was written by some psychiatrist.* I remember all these Judy Blume books—oh, my

* Richard A. Gardner, *The Boys and Girls Book About Divorce* (New York: Bantam, 1971).

God, all these horrible things happening! It was just so much fiction! I had a friend whose parents were getting divorced, and he was wondering how he should feel. I told him it wasn't normal to feel like that.

QUENTIN: You should feel the way you feel. And if that's the way you feel, that's how you should feel, and you shouldn't feel guilty for feeling good about it or bad about it. When it comes to your parents getting divorced, you really don't have any obligation to feel any emotion at all. Because it's *their* problem.

PETER: The custody battle still affects your life.

QUENTIN: Yes, but you don't have to feel bad. And in our case, there wasn't a custody battle. My mother didn't want custody, so my stepmother just didn't do anything.

PETER: My mother didn't file for custody because she knew she couldn't win.

QUENTIN: But we had problems with the deals about custody. That was really hard to understand. She wanted my father to pay for round trips for us to go out there once a weekend, or something like that, something really crazy. And there were other problems.

PETER: I remember on the day the custody battles—everything—were finished, my father smiled and said, "I'm free!" And I remember thinking, "Good, now he's happy. And he has no debts or obligations, and he won't have any more custody battles, and no one's upset at him —he's free!"

QUENTIN: After that it was still pretty messed up, because we had to see our mother once a week. We had a good time, but it got awkward sometimes. She'd want to talk about stuff that was uncomfortable. I was kind of afraid to see her. I really didn't want to see her. Then we came back to North America, and I really kind of began to hate her. She was a representation of something that I couldn't control, and I didn't like that. She's still in South America.

PETER: When we got back to the U.S. we stayed at our grandparents' for about a month. My grandmother wanted to know what we were going to call my stepmother. We had this gigantic argument about what to call her. First of all we called her Ellie, and she hated that. But we didn't understand it.

QUENTIN: It was all very confusing. She wanted us to call her Mom. Now it would be the only thing I would ever think of calling her, because she *is* my mother as far as I'm concerned.

PETER: But back then, I was kind of scared that if I did anything wrong, even the simplest thing, she'd be upset at me, and I couldn't understand what I was doing wrong.

QUENTIN: This was the main reason that it took me so long to call her Mom. I thought that the first time I'd call her Mom—this is the truth, my own selfish reason—I thought she'd start crying, and it would be like this big happy corny scene. And that was the main reason that I didn't want to call her Mom. I was worried that everyone would start crying! [Laughs.] And that I'd be sitting there bawling.

PETER: I remember my parents got married . . .

QUENTIN: Yes, they weren't married then, and that made it kind of confusing. But she wanted us to call her Mom! So then they got married, and then, fine! It wasn't really the wedding, but the wedding gave me the excuse —okay, now I can do it.

PETER: Our parents went on their honeymoon, and our grandparents stayed with us. They said, "Okay, as soon as they get back, call her Mom." And we made a sign. They wanted it to say, "Welcome back. Congratulations, Mom and Dad." And we put some corny thing like

"Welcome home, we need our allowances." My grand-mother got really upset. So we finally put what they wanted, and I said, "Hi, Mom," and she stared at me and said, "Oh, hi, Peter."

QUENTIN: I just remember it was gifts and "Mom." It wasn't a really cheerful jubilation. That was cool. A lot of times people say it's easier to start something than it is to quit, but sometimes it's a lot harder to start something. Especially big changes like that. Then I was very scared of changing things.

Did you ever see a play called *The Curious Savage?* It's about an insane asylum. This woman who is sane is put into the asylum with all these people with their com-plexes and things. One of them has this big guilt com-plex, because he was the only person in his squadron who wasn't killed. Another one went crazy because his job was taken away, and he was replaced by a computer. Another one thinks this doll was her child. And another who is pretty ugly thinks she is gorgeous. They don't go to sleep at night because they're afraid. When you go to sleep, today ends and tomorrow begins, and they're afraid of tomorrow. They stay up all night, so that today, which is the only certainty to them, will be there the next day when they get out of bed. So that signifies that change is a very scary thing to people. I think I'm a little bit better equipped to handle changes like that. But then I wasn't.

PETER: Quentin felt upset. I didn't.

QUENTIN: Peter didn't care if we called her Bananas.

PETER: Yes, that's a quote of mine. I didn't care. I could have called her Bananahead.

QUENTIN: Peter has always been very easygoing about that kind of stuff. He wants to sit in the front seat of the car, and he wants the window seat on the plane, a bigger piece of cake, and stupid stuff like that . . .

PETER: Yeah!

QUENTIN: But the monumental stuff doesn't bother him, usually.

PETER: When I was really young, whenever I was faced by a gigantic decision, like who are you going to stay with, your dad or mom, I always said, "Well, Quentin will tell me."

QUENTIN: Yes, usually I was there to make the decision.

PETER: In an argument I would never talk. I would just sit there, and Quentin would talk for me. Quentin was a pretty nice big brother. He was my idol from when I was in kindergarten to about fifth grade. Everything I did was because Quentin did. My favorite color used to be red until Quentin said his was blue, so I changed mine to blue. But I've kind of grown out of that now.

QUENTIN: It's more like I'm giving advice rather than his copying me.

QUENTIN: We see my mother once a year. We meet her in some neutral place, like New York. She goes there from South America.

PETER: Because my dad says we're not old enough to fly to South America alone.

QUENTIN: So we meet her somewhere for about two weeks, three weeks. She comes alone. The rest of the time I'm not worried about her. She can take care of herself. I'm concerned about her drinking, though. Every once in a while she'll drink till she passes out. It's hard for me to do anything five thousand miles away, but I don't feel tense or constantly concerned about her.

So things are settled. Except every once in a while something happens. There are places in the tropics where they have monsoons. Everything is really nice for a while and the sun is out, then all of a sudden BOOM!

The storm comes. Then it goes away. It's kind of like that. Every time I think it's going to be calm again, something else comes up. We thought everything was cool—calm—then Ellie said she wanted to adopt us. Which is fine. I really don't mind one way or another. If she adopts us fine, if not, fine.

PETER: I kind of want her to adopt us. This year I had my appendix out. It was almost a life-or-death situation at one point, because the school nurse diagnosed me wrong. My appendix burst before I got to the hospital, and they had to operate on me immediately.

QUENTIN: And Dad was out of town.

PETER: No, Dad was there, but my stepmother signed the papers, which was kind of illegal, since she's not my true adopted mother. So she wants us to get adopted, partly for that reason, mostly because she loves us. My mother in South America, natural mother as some of the psychiatrists call it, says, "I could stand giving you up to your father because it was a great sacrifice and you needed it, but I can't give you away like that to another woman. I love you too much to do that."

QUENTIN: No, it wasn't like that. I'm going to use another example: Muhammad Ali. He's a boxer, and he beats up people for a living, it's what he does to make money. But when they wanted to draft him and send him off to Vietnam, he said, "That's where I draw the line. I'm not going to kill any Vietnamese." That's kind of what she did. She said, "I'll live five thousand miles away from them, and I'll see them once a year, but I draw the line at giving them up for adoption."

I understand. She wants the big slice of cake. So whatever happens is going to happen. Selfishly speaking, if the adoption comes through, my life can only get better. So whatever happens, it's not going to be a monumental change for the worse. I don't really have any control over the situation, and I'd rather stay neutral. I'm very happy the way I am.

PETER: Yeah. From my experience of divorce, divorce is livable. People say that it's the end of the world, that divorce ends a chapter in your life. But it also starts a new, better one.

QUENTIN: What it is, is another change. Or it's a kind of an end and a beginning. People are always scared of ends. The only end that people celebrate as a general rule is the end of a war. And people don't see this as an end of a war, they see it as an end of a marriage. A marriage is like a little bird: you can't squeeze it too tight, and you can't separate its two wings. If people would see divorce as the end of a fight or a war, I think it wouldn't be such a problem. But they see it as the end of a marriage, a little bird or something.

PETER: Yes, but what if they say "family" instead of "marriage"?

QUENTIN: The end of a family?

PETER: Yes, though it's not.

QUENTIN AND PETER (in unison): It *is* the end of a family, but . . .

PETER: It's the beginning of a different family!

QUENTIN: I believe in the family. A family is terrific! Some of my best friends are family. [Laughs.] I wouldn't be here if it weren't for my family.

PETER: I don't think my dad could have made it without my stepmother. I think my dad is a lot happier with my stepmother.

QUENTIN: Oh, yes, *they're* a lot happier. And in terms of me, it's also better for me.

PETER: It's better having two parents than one. People say that if it's a bad family it's better just to have one parent. That's true, if there is constant fighting going on.

But if you have two happy parents who are willing to take care of you, it's great.

QUENTIN: Two heads are better than one, I agree with him.

PETER: I've got a little advice for anyone going through their parents' divorce. The way I survived, handled all the guilt trips, and "Oh, do you love me?"—oh, yes, both sides asked that question a lot. The thing to do is mainly think one thought. If someone is talking to you, stare at the light switch until your eyes start to bulge out of your head. Try not to talk much. Say, "Yes, that's true, but also . . ." And try to be on everyone's side, if possible. There's the old story of the bat and two armies. The beasts and the birds were having a fight, and the bat went with the beasts. And then the beasts were losing, and he went with the birds. And after the war, everyone hated the bat. But in an argument, don't say "Yes, I agree with you totally," and then in the middle of the argument say "No, I agree with her (or him) more."

QUENTIN: You see, there *were* arguments, and we were asked to take sides.

PETER: Yes. "Who do you think is best?" Or "Who do you think is right?" It didn't go on for very long, though.

QUENTIN: Not really. But when it comes to Mom or Dad, don't take sides! Tell them that. You have no obligation to take a side; all you'll do is hurt their feelings. Just remain totally neutral.

PETER: If you think one person is obviously better, then take that side. But if you love them both, don't take sides or else you'll wind up hating the other person.

QUENTIN: Or the other person will wind up hating you.

PETER: And you don't want that to happen.

QUENTIN: And if you have a big brother, just listen to him!

PETER: Yeah. [Laughs.] I remember listening to everything my father and stepmother said, listening to them willingly, and then I started to hate my mother in South America.

QUENTIN: Yes, don't take one side. If you feel you have to take one side, get out and be by yourself for a while and go over everything each party said, and sift it and weigh it, go through everything that they said, and then begin to form an opinion.

PETER: Over the years, the number of people getting divorced has increased. It started off way back when I was really young, about one kid in the crowd had divorced parents. One out of every two marriages doesn't turn out well. I saw that somewhere. I don't think of divorce as a horrible thing that only the freak kids have. I think of divorce as being one of the guys.

QUENTIN: I know what you mean.

PETER: Divorce used to mean you'd be an outcast not having two parents. There didn't use to be single parents. Now all that has changed.

Charlie and Jeff

You Gotta Stand Up for Yourself

Charlie, fourteen, and Jeff, thirteen, are friends attending high school in a small, Atlantic coast resort town. They thought it would be more comfortable if they teamed up for the interview. Charlie's parents have been reconciled after a two-year separation. Charlie is angry at his father's behavior and resents his father's preference for his older brother. Jeff, in a more thoughtful, slightly wistful manner, has resigned himself to his parents' divorce. He has chosen to live with his father, to whom he is deeply attached, and does not envy his brothers' life with his mother. Jeff shows he has been deeply wounded by his family's breakup, but he is struggling to resolve his feelings about it.

CHARLIE: My parents split up because my mom told my dad he just had to leave. They didn't really get divorced, but they were separated for two years. My mom had kicked him out because he didn't have a good job. He did get a good job, and last summer he started living back at the house again. And they seem okay again.

My little sister cried all the time he was away because she really didn't know it was all for the best. Every night my mom would give her a bedtime kiss, and she'd say, "How come Daddy's not here?" My older brother wanted my dad to come back, too, but he understood. And so did I, I guess, but it was hard not having a father. We both missed him a lot.

We made out pretty well while he was gone. We all did different chores. My big brother was working. I took care of my sister while my mom was at work, and I helped out about a lot of things. I did the cooking. I cut lawns and gave Mom some money. Also my father paid some money while he was away. Mom and Dad talked to each other. It wasn't like they were enemies.

My mother didn't really talk to us about it, but we all knew why it was happening, because we had heard them fighting in the middle of the night. But there was never any explanation given to us by either of our parents. Mom came to me and my brother and said, "I guess you know why your dad isn't living here anymore." And we said, "Yes." And she said, "No more to be said."

Dad came to see us on the weekends. He wanted to come back and everything, but deep down inside he knew it was the best thing for him. Before, he didn't want to get a better job or anything. Mom forced him to. He had had a job, but at a very low salary. He'd keep on saying that he was going to look for a job in the city, but then he wouldn't.

I don't know how I feel about my dad anymore. He's weird now, not like part of the family. Look what he's done to my mom! My mom was in research, and she quit that so she could have us. It had been sixteen years, and she didn't want to, but she had to go back to work because Dad wasn't making enough money. Mom must have been through a lot of pain. I will never forgive him for what he did.

He and I don't really talk much. He doesn't hit me, but he yells at me all the time, because he's closer to my brother. If my brother and I are fighting, and Dad doesn't like it, I'll be the one who gets grounded. But I just say to Mom, "I'm not listening to him. I'm not grounded, and if he doesn't let me go, I'm going to tell him off." And Mom says, "All right. You can go out." My mom knows he just picks on me.

Mom caters to me a little over my brother because of my dad. I don't care. It's just a mess. My brother and I don't talk to each other much either. We all got along pretty well before too—until about the last six months before my mom threw my dad out. We'd all go play basketball, go to the beach, everything. It'll probably change again. I'm just really upset after what my dad did to my mother, that's about all.

Besides, he doesn't act right. He tries to make like he never left. He tries to do all these chores around the house. As though he's trying to work himself back, you know? He says, "You guys want to go for ice cream now?" He makes me sick!

JEFF: My parents got divorced about three years ago. My dad is remarried now. He met Doris, my stepmother, when I was living in New Orleans with my mother and brothers. I decided to move back here by myself because I didn't like New Orleans and my mother.

When my parents separated, I didn't want my dad to leave. I wanted to go with him. Dad said, "I can't let you go with me." I was crying, but I had to go with my mother. It was hard for me when they first got divorced; it was a real big change. Then when my dad got remarried, I didn't really like my stepmother that much. Everybody says they can't see their father or mother with anybody else. Finally, as I got older, I could make my own decision and I decided to go with my dad. I'm much happier now.

New Orleans is not my cup of tea. Everything is hot, and there are drugs and everything. I almost got into it, and I didn't want to. I was always depressed. I don't like my mom at all. My brothers stayed there. I wished they lived here, too, but they don't want to live here. They're older than I am, and I don't know if they're doing it because they want to or because they feel they have to stay with my mother. Because she isn't able to get along by herself.

My mother thinks she and I get along, but I don't. I just don't like her now. I don't know, maybe I never did, but I thought I did. And then when they got divorced, it came out that I really didn't. I don't think I ever trusted her. She always caused problems. Even after their breakup, she always wanted to pick a fight with my dad because of my stepmother. Once I came here for a vacation, and when I got back to New Orleans, she gave me the third degree: "How was Doris?"—real sarcastic. I'd say, "Mom, don't ask me that." She'd say, "Does she get close?" And I couldn't say anything, because every time she'd get mad at me she'd say, "You don't love me." She'd get all angry and tell me to go live with my father. One time I said I'd try that, and she said she was only kidding!

She still gets upset about the divorce. My bar mitzvah is coming up soon and she talks about how she would go if she had a boyfriend or a husband. But she doesn't, so she wouldn't feel right, seeing my stepmother with my dad at the bar mitzvah.

It was hard getting used to living with my stepsisters.

I'd hear them call my dad Dad, and I'd get a little shaky. He's *my* dad! But now it doesn't bother me that much. They probably went through the same thing, because their parents got divorced too. And my younger stepsister, she has a stepmother also—she doesn't like her stepmother. When she was a little younger, about two years ago, she loved her dad—she was always talking about it. But then she learned how bad he is. She doesn't see him hardly. So they're happier with their mother—my stepmother.

It was hard getting used to my stepmother too. I'd get all upset when she tried to act like my mother. I'd get mad and think, "Why is she doing that?" And she was really only trying to help. I took it as if she was trying to be mean to me. So I thought I didn't like her, but I do. It was a matter of getting used to her. I have really changed about that.

CHARLIE: Does your mother let your older brothers get away with a lot of stuff?

JEFF: Yes, she does.

CHARLIE: Maybe that could be a reason they want to stay with her. Maybe your dad wouldn't let them do things.

JEFF: Yes, they'd have a party every night if she weren't there. And if she found out, she'd just yell and scream for five minutes, and then she'd stop. She'd just forget about it. They'd talk her into not getting mad. They hardly do any work around the house, and she can't do anything because they don't listen to her.

CHARLIE: So that's one reason they stay down there.

JEFF: Yes. But I feel I have the better part of the bargain even if they get away with a lot of stuff. I have a better life. If they're going to stay there, they'll probably screw up because of my mother. So I don't resent them. I resent my mother.

CHARLIE: My brother gets away with more stuff, too, but I don't resent him either. I resent my father because of all he did to my mother.

JEFF: Lots of older guys get away with stuff. If it's just the mother and some big kid, the mother isn't going to be able to tell the kid what to do, because the kid will just say, "Too bad!" My mother feels they're going to leave for college real soon, and it doesn't pay to yell at them.

CHARLIE: But if they were up here, your dad would probably give them a hard time.

JEFF: Yes. I think he's the better discipliner.

CHARLIE: My mom tells my dad what to do. She's the stronger one in my family. Dad's such a wimp! If he tells me I'm grounded, I say, "Shut the hell up," and I just keep on walking. And he can't object to my talking like that. If he tried to hit me, my mom would kill him. My mom would beat the crap out of him. Your dad is different. If your brothers were with your dad they wouldn't act that way, because your dad would whale them.

JEFF: And my mom wouldn't have any say. Yet if my dad had stayed with my mother, it would be a mess. The way they were, they had to separate. They weren't right for each other. It probably would be the way it is now. I probably wouldn't like my mom because of what she was doing. So I think it was a good idea all this happened.

CHARLIE: Me too. I think so too.

JEFF: It's a matter of luck, but also you gotta stand up for yourself.

CHARLIE: You gotta keep your pride and dignity, because if you don't, then you fall apart.

JEFF: And if that happens, then everybody's going to fall apart.

CHARLIE: You've got to keep your cool and hang in there, because sometimes that helps.

JEFF: That's right. I feel as if I was a support to my dad, because he always wanted one of his sons to come and live with him, now that he lives in a new house and stuff. If I hadn't come to live with him, or one of my brothers, he would have always been depressed. He always says, "If you don't want to live here, fine. I love you anyway." But I know inside he wants at least one of us, if not all of us.

CHARLIE: Does your dad favor you over your stepsisters?

JEFF: No, not really. He'll get mad at me more than at my sisters. He'll hit me a couple of times, 'cause he can't hit my sisters. My stepmother won't let him. But my stepsisters will get on his nerves more than I will.

CHARLIE: Does your stepmother always get mad at you?

JEFF: No, she'll get mad at my stepsisters more. But she's starting to give me more of a pep talk here and there. Before she wouldn't, because she wasn't my mother—I *think* she felt like that—and she couldn't do anything because I'd get real mad and she didn't want me to leave for my dad's sake. So she just kept it cool for a little while. Now she knows that if I get excited and threaten to move, I'm not going to move. In fact, my dad said that if I move back with my mother, I can't move back here. It's one or the other.

I know I'm not going to go back to New Orleans. The whole problem is my mother.

CHARLIE: And in my family, it's my father.

Rachel and David

We Didn't Know Anyone Whose Parents Were Divorced

Rachel, fifteen, and David, thirteen, are sister and brother and asked to be interviewed together. They attend the senior and junior high schools in a suburban town. Since their parents split up two years ago, their father no longer communicates with the children. While both kids seem cautious and reserved, they quickly reveal their feelings about their father. Rachel is angry and says she is beginning to feel indifferent about him. David, on the other hand, grieves about his loss and still wishes he could see his father. Neither as yet seems to have resolved his or her feelings.

DAVID: Our parents first told us they were going to separate during the summer two years ago. I was eleven and Rachel was thirteen. We were living in H——————. My mom left, and my sister, my dad, and I stayed on there about a month, I think. Then my mom found a job and a house here, and we moved here. My dad stayed back in H——————— for a while, and then he moved to New York. He's there now. We've been with our mom ever since.

In the beginning we saw him sometimes, but I haven't seen him in a long, long time. That isn't because I don't want to. He just doesn't come around. At first I was sad and scared because I didn't know what was going to happen. Where I was going to live. About the dogs. Just what it was going to be like, after. I don't remember how long it took to get over that or when it happened. I just stopped feeling that way. I don't feel this has ruined my life or anything. I've just learned how to get along with the situation.

RACHEL: I remember feeling shocked when they told us. In some ways I knew it was coming. It was the general atmosphere—it was tense. But it was totally different actually hearing it from them and knowing it was going to happen! I didn't know anyone whose parents were divorced, and it was just weird to think my parents were. I didn't know what it was going to be like, and I didn't know where we were going to live, and with what parent, and what was going to change and . . . I just didn't understand why it was happening! I did have a preference about which parent to live with. I preferred my mom. I just felt more comfortable. I get along better with her.

DAVID: And I wanted my dad. We had more in common. We like to do the same things. But it didn't work out that I could stay with him.

RACHEL: Neither of us knew kids who had divorced parents, not to talk to. It's different in this town, though.

DAVID: I feel more comfortable here. About a quarter of my friends' parents are divorced or being separated.

RACHEL: But I remember then, there was no one I

really knew. It probably would have made it easier. I wished there was someone besides a parent—someone older—to talk to. We did go to see a child psychiatrist, but I never wanted to talk to him. I still don't feel ready to share *all* my problems with him.

DAVID: I feel uncomfortable talking to somebody that you don't really know.

RACHEL: I felt like he was poking into our business. He had no right. I didn't want to tell him anything. I think I *might* talk to somebody now if I had problems—to a psychiatrist. I think two years makes a difference. I think it just takes time. It seems like they've always been separated now. We're used to this way of living.

DAVID: They haven't actually got a divorce yet. My dad won't contribute anything for us. He just doesn't. My mom would prefer that he did. It's not a happy situation.

RACHEL: It makes me mad! I don't talk to him, because he doesn't come around, but I think it's his responsibility. I have no idea why he doesn't want to.

DAVID: I don't either.

RACHEL: He just doesn't take responsibility, and that's part of the reason why I don't talk to him, try to call him up.

DAVID: He never even calls *us* up. He sends cards on Christmas and holidays.

RACHEL: And I don't think that situation will change as time goes by. I think it will get worse, if anything. I think it will just drift and drift. Now I don't care any more, but in the beginning it was like going from a father who was always there to just nothing. That's weird. I think it's pretty sad to lose a father like that, but that's the way it happens.

DAVID: I think it might be easier once the divorce is finally settled. Because then everything will be clear. Like money. What he has to contribute, instead of my mom calling him up and asking him for money. Not that she does that anymore.

RACHEL: She only discusses our financial situation a little bit, but I feel secure about money. But moving down here—that was upsetting—a big change! Different schools and all. Changing friends. You don't want to have to change *anything* at the same time your family's breaking up. Especially friends!

DAVID: If I had to go through this again, I'd say maybe parents should settle as quickly as possible. That's really it. The faster they could do it, the less pain it would be to the kids.

RACHEL: And I think maybe not having to switch where you live or schools, that would be a help too. I don't think there's any way you could do it perfectly, but I think anything like that would be helpful. Mom just wanted to get out of the area where we lived before. I would have preferred it if she had stuck around. Now it doesn't mean so much.

DAVID: Now I like it here better.

RACHEL: I do, too, but then I remember wishing we could stay and everything wouldn't have to change. It's so confusing. Everything's fine one day, and the next day it's not. It took two years to get rid of those feelings. They're still going on just a little, and for a year, year and a half, they were tough to handle. It's just a way of life now. I think it would have been worse if they had tried to stay together and had been living together with all those tensions. It hurt then to have them split, but now it's just more comfortable. I think it was a good solution for them. I think if they were unhappy together it would have made everything unhappy.

DAVID: I agree.

RACHEL: But I feel a lot of anger about our father.

DAVID: Yes, a lot. I'm just kind of living with that.

RACHEL: There's not much you can do. That's just the way it is. I told him this, and it just didn't make an impression on him. He doesn't respond in any way. He wasn't always that way. Not really. Or maybe he was, but we just didn't see it. I think the separation brought it out. He can't handle things. He runs from them instead.

DAVID: I agree with that, but I would like him to come around so that I could see him and be with him sometimes, at least.

RACHEL: I'm getting very indifferent about him. I don't know how he'd feel if he knew that. It certainly would be a shock if they made up!

DAVID: That is never going to happen! Even though I have kind of secret wishes that it would.

RACHEL: I don't!

DAVID: I know it's impossible. I still don't know or understand why they split up. But I don't feel it had anything to do with us kids.

RACHEL: If you'd asked me a year ago how I felt, it would have made a difference. I don't think I'd have had that much to say. Now that it has been two years, I think everything has kind of settled in my mind, and I pretty much understand why it happened and what's happening now. But if you'd talked to me a year ago, I would have had a lot more anger and been more upset simply because it all would have been fresh. Now I don't feel it at all.

DAVID: I'm sorry not to have a complete family. I feel families in general are a good idea, and I plan to have one when I grow up. But I hope *my* family works!

Jeannie

A Fresh Start

Jeannie is fourteen and looks strained and malnourished. She has run away from a life with her mother that finally became intolerable, she says. She describes long years of loneliness and instances of harsh treatment. Still somewhat dazed by her hitchhiking journey and her encounter with the police, Jeannie has found refuge at Harbor House, a hostel for runaways in a medium-sized eastern city. She is relieved and excited at the prospect of finding both a suitable foster home and the solution to her problems.

Monday I left Indiana because they were going to send me back home. My mom is a prostitute, and there is no way I can live with a prostitute any longer. So I left the Ark, a hostel for runaways where I'd been staying, and headed south on foot with my friend. Just before we got to the highway, a guy in a pickup truck stopped for us.

He had a CB, and we were talking on it when we got on the highway. It was my girlfriend who had the guts to start a conversation with another truck driver. She says, "Where are you going?" He says, "Philadelphia." And she goes, "Can we come?" He says, "Well, let's stop and talk about it." So we stopped at the nearest rest area, and the guy in the pickup truck took off. The big rig arrived, we got in, and on our way we went! Just like that! I had a bag of clothes with me, two pairs of pants, a couple of shirts, my winter coat. It was the first time I ever hitch-hiked. It wasn't really scary once I did it. I had just been worried that we'd get picked up by the wrong person.

So we stopped here overnight with the truck driver on our way to Philadelphia. My friend is still with him, I guess. But I got in a conversation with a lady in the Laundromat while I was doing laundry. I told her I was from Indiana and that I had come here with a truck driver, and she called the cops. She was concerned.

My girlfriend was in the motel sleeping. The Laundro-mat was right across the highway. This lady asked if she could drop me off at the motel, and I said, "Sure."

The next thing you know, I'm sitting in the rig talking on the CB, listening to the radio, and a cop pulls up. I said, "Oh, gosh!" I turned off the CB, turned off the radio, got out, locked the door—it took forever because it was so hard to turn—and he goes, "Hi, Jeannie!" I turned around and said, "Who?" Acting dumb, like I wasn't that person. But after a minute, I looked at him and said, "Okay, hold on, you know who I am." It was the lady. I had told her. She had been concerned about me. Right now I am glad she called in for me. I'm really glad! Because my whole life has turned around. She only knew about me, and I didn't tell on my friend. I figured if she wanted to get in trouble further down the line, it's her problem. I've got to deal with mine. One of these days I'll see her again and explain what happened.

The cop said, "Where are you from?" I told him. He goes, "What are you doing here?" And I told him. "My mom is a prostitute and I ran away from her, because I couldn't cope with living with her." The police took me to the police station, and I just broke down in tears. I told them I couldn't go back home because of my mom. They told me they could understand, that it wasn't the kind of life they'd expect me to have either. They told me they wouldn't send me back. They told me about Harbor House and brought me here. They were the first people who ever tried to help me get away. That was a surprise, because nobody before would help me get away. The Indiana police wouldn't have helped me get away!

So here I am, and it's really nice here. You get the help you need and want. Usually right now I'd break down in tears, talking about my mom, but now I've learned to cope with saying it right out to people.

My life has really been hard. My mother and father were divorced after I was born. My mother lives in E————, and my father lives in I————. I don't know him. I once called him and asked him if I could come stay with him for a couple of days, and he said, "No. Bye." That hurt me a lot. I've never lived with him at all.

There are six in the family, except I was the only one at home. Both my sisters left when I was seven. I was raised with three brothers, and they were into drugs and alcohol and stuff. And that's another thing. If you're raised wrong, you get into all that yourself. I did, but not as bad as my brothers did. I've experienced drugs, most teenagers do. I don't like it. It's not for me. And I just don't like it there because of the surroundings. It's just not the environment that you want. I don't like my school because I have all the teachers my brothers and sisters had. They put me down for what the others have done. We live in a pretty large city, but it's hard to go to school in another district than your own.

Anyway, now I'm going to live with my aunt. It's all decided. I'm leaving tonight at six o'clock on the bus for Indiana. I came on Tuesday, and now on Thursday things have already turned around. I called my aunt because I needed to go somewhere. It was either stay here or go to my home state, and I'd rather go there because I don't know anybody here. I need my relatives' support really badly right now.

I'm going to be changing schools and the whole bit. I won't have all the heavy things I've had from my brothers and sisters all my life. My aunt is looking forward to having me. I'll be getting there tomorrow. She has two kids. The youngest one is sixteen—she and I got to be really close last summer, so it's going to be fun. They've got an exchange student living with them right now, too, and they live near a lake. So it's going to be nice.

My mom didn't think too highly of the idea. She wants me home. But she's not that worried about me, because she knows I'm in good hands. One of the counselors here was talking to her and said it was either I go stay with a relative, or I'd go back on the run. And one day I might end up dead and raped in an alley. So she went along with it.

My aunt works with juveniles back in Indiana. They're going to find a foster home for me—one that suits *me*, not my mother, and that suits *me!* So the stay with my aunt will be temporary. She's got a lot of connections, but it just depends on how long it takes.

I love my mother, but I hate her too. Because of the things she does. Everybody else knows she's a prostitute, but my sisters and brothers think I'm cracked and are trying to get me to see a psychiatrist. It's my mom who's cracked and should be seeing a psychiatrist! She brings men home! She admitted it to my counselor here. But she would not admit it to the police, because she can get put into jail for prostitution.

I also don't want to live with my mother because I get hit quite a bit. But that's not the big reason. I've just had it with her. I've put up with a lot, being the only kid left in the house. I have to do this, I have to do that. We've got a roomer. He doesn't clean up his mess. He accuses me of stealing things. He walks in my bedroom, and sometimes in the summer I sleep nude. He's looking for cigarettes, because I smoke. It's not right when you have to lock your door! And the tenant who's got the apartment in front, she's like my mother. She tells me what to do, and if I don't do it, I get yelled at. If I come home five minutes late, Audrey will be sitting there at the table, and my mom will say, "Well, where have you been?" I tell her, and Audrey will say, "Ground her for a couple of weeks." My mom will do it! She doesn't listen to me, she won't. I tell her I don't think it's right that I have to do so much. She says, "It's not your choice. I tell you to do something, you'd better do it or you're going to get your butt beat." That's not right either!

I don't have any friends back home. Everybody knows my mom is a prostitute. It's not easy for me to make friends because of all the rumors. My name carries awfully fast. Which I don't like.

But now I'll have a fresh start. I feel good about taking a real step now, because I know I'm doing something right for myself. I don't think I'm doing something right for my mom, because I'm hurting her. But she has hurt me for thirteen years.

This has been a good experience for me at this place, but I'm anxious to leave and get there. I'm glad there was a place for me to go. Because if I went to someplace like the Ark, I would have to go home eventually. And I don't want to go home. I want to go to a foster home to get away from my mom. I know I'll have to go through counseling. That I can handle, but not living with her. You know, this is my turnover from twelve to fourteen, and it's really hard, because I've got to learn how to adapt to things. Different changes in my body and stuff, and she will not listen to me. She doesn't know what is going on with me because she will not listen. Sometimes I'm afraid even to say something to her. If I do something wrong, I'm afraid. It's not really good when I go home.

I want to go to counseling, but I didn't like the counselor I had at the Ark, who was saying nothing but "I think it can work out at home. It will work out." He was trying to say that my mother can change her life-style, but she's been doing this for God knows how long! My grandparents tried to tell me when I was ten that my mom was a prostitute, and I didn't know what it meant. Now I've found out. So it's kind of hard, but I'm learning to cope with it. My best friend knows, but I don't think her parents do. If they were to find out about my mom, I would never see my friend again. And I've known her all my life. It's nice to have somebody around like that. We get into fights, say, one day at noon, and by three o'clock we'll be buddy-buddies again. It's kind of hard to hate anybody you're close to. Even my mother.

The other night when I arrived here I kept saying, "I hate her! I hate her! I hate her!" Then I lay down and went to sleep. When I woke up, I realized I didn't hate her. I'm just really angry! There's no hate in it right now, it's just my feelings for her are negative. They have been for the past year, but I do love her.

Laura

Some People Just Don't Want Their Kids

Laura, a social worker, is director of Harbor House, the hostel for runaways and other troubled young people where Jeannie (p. 43) and Karen (p. 61) found help. The hostel is a private institution, although it receives contributions from the county and the state. Most young people hear of it by word of mouth; some are referred by schools or other social agencies. The hostel also advertises on the local radio stations. There is live-in space for about a dozen people, although many opt for help on an outclient basis. There are nine trained professional counselors, each of whom works with only about three clients at a time. Unlike the many agencies that must assign much larger caseloads, Harbor House can offer each young person a lot of close attention.

It seems like parents are all so busy that they don't have enough time to spend with their kids. Kids are rebelling against both parents' working, even if right now both parents *have* to work. It's hard on the kids, but it's hard on the parents too. A mother who has to work all day and then come home and get dinner and do housework does not have much time to spend with her kids. The kids are feeling that a lot.

Also, younger parents seem more self-centered than those in previous generations. A parent seems to be saying "I have to find myself, and I can't give to you unless I know myself, and I'm going to do this and that for *me.*" That's serious. They want to do their own thing first, and it's so easy just to give up responsibilities and leave rather than to work out problems.

I once said to my own mother, "You've been married for forty-five years! How did you do that?" She told me, "You know, we had plenty of problems, but we worked them out. There were weeks that I didn't talk to your father because I was mad at him, but it worked out. We had a commitment that it *would* work out." I think younger people have lost that. It's too easy to get mad and say "This is it!" and leave. I see this pattern both among well-to-do people and among people on welfare. The parents who don't work are not spending the time with their kids.

Usually it's just the mother I work with, because the father is out of the home. She's just too busy with her life and her own friends. She wants to stay home and hang out and watch TV soap operas and not really be involved with the kids' schoolwork and activities. So many parents don't know their kids' friends, don't know where their kids go after school, and don't hold them accountable for what they do.

And some of the people we work with honestly just don't want their kids. They never did, and there's nothing we can do to change it. Kids get a real sense of that. A *real* sense, and they start feeling like they're not worth anything. Their parents refuse to come in and work with us. They are quick to say "Send them to relatives or let the youth authorities take them. I can't control my kids." It's often just an excuse. Sometimes the kids are being played off as pawns between a mother and a father who are separating and using the kids to get back at one another.

Soon kids show their anger and resentment through their behavior. Usually there are a lot of school problems. Disrespect for teachers, refusal to work, not going to school. In extreme cases we find bed-wetting, even in older teenagers who are embarrassed by it.

A lot of kids steal or get into trouble because they want attention. Or they just get into the wrong crowd, and they feel good with the crowd because they're accepted. They'd do anything the crowd wants them to do. We see a lot of drug and alcohol use. There are other reasons behind it, but it's easy to see why those kids love that high—they don't have to think about anything else that might be bothering them.

Parents get into trouble too. I work a lot with the Toughlove movement. That's a parents' support group for people who are having problems with their teenage kids. Basically, Toughlove will teach parents not to confuse leniency with love. Parents are very lenient with their kids. They aren't making them responsible for their actions. A boy will have cursed out a parent, but the next day the parent will go ahead and give the boy his allowance. A Toughlove member would say, "Your kid doesn't deserve that allowance. He was disrespectful to you. Don't give it to him. And don't feel bad about it."

So many times the *parents* feel bad. They think *they're* doing something wrong, it's all *their* fault! This is particularly true of single mothers. They want so much to be friends—especially with their daughters—but in adolescence kids don't want their mothers as friends. It isn't until the mother realizes there are going to be a couple of shaky years in adolescence that things get better. They can't be their kids' friends. They can't buy them off with material things. They're going to have to be mothers, and they're going to have to put restrictions on their kids—set rules and stick by them. But so often they don't. They just feel guilty. A lot of single mothers say, "Well, she doesn't have a father. I have to do all this alone. It's hard, and I don't like the responsibility." It *is* hard!

A lot of family problems are due to unemployment. A kid will come to our door who has run away from home because his parents have just been fighting and fighting. Or the kid's father is changing. "He's nasty, he's mean, he never wants me to leave the house. He's always complaining. I can never get money from him." Usually those fathers will come in and talk about the problem. Either they're worried sick about losing their job, or they don't have a job and are looking frantically for one. That causes problems, not only between husband and wife, but between parents and kids. Kids see everything that is going on in the house, and they can feel the tension. They don't like it and they leave.

There really isn't a "runaway personality." We've had such a diversity of kids! We get them from upper-class suburbia and from the poorest areas of the inner city. And different problems. Sometimes we get kids who have been molested, abused, or who are the victims of incest. We get a lot of kids whose parents have alcohol problems. In most cases there is a lack of communication between the parents and the kids. The kid doesn't know how to tell his parents things, and the parent doesn't know how to talk to the kid, maybe about school problems. Mainly the kids come here, but a parent may also come and say "Will you talk with me? I think I'm going nuts with my kid." Or "I'm having a problem with my son. He won't come in and talk to you." We usually encourage the parents themselves to come in. "Why don't you come in and we'll see what we can do. We'll tell you what options are open to you as a parent."

Sometimes it's just a matter of a kid coming once for a talk and then going away. Sometimes we get kids who've been thrown out of school and are afraid to go home and tell their parents. We try to get them to face it. "Hey, look, you probably will get punished, but you deserve it. You got thrown out! So you've got to take the consequences. Don't think you can come here and hide. You just can't do that." Usually they end up going home and facing it.

Sometimes it takes us a long time to realize exactly what the problem is. We've had kids come through this program three or four times. And each time they come through, we find out something we didn't know before. Maybe by the fourth time we have a clear picture of what's going on and can start discussing what pattern we're seeing and what we can recommend. Kids don't come in and say, "This is my problem, and I want you to help me." We have to fish it out of them. And out of parents, too, sometimes.

If a kid or a parent really doesn't want help, or they don't really want to change, they're not going to follow through no matter how many referrals or recommendations we make. Sometimes parents and kids just want to complain, but they don't want to put energy into changing what's happening in their lives. We can't *make* them want to change.

There really are people who seem incorrigible. There are kids who simply don't go by their parents' rules. And it's not that there's anything wrong with the family life, they just refuse to listen. But sometimes there *is* something wrong with the family. The kids are acting out, and they're being incorrigible, but there's a reason. And you can get at that so much more easily, whatever it is, if the people involved are willing to talk about it. The most difficult client is the one who simply won't listen. "My parents are wrong, they're old-fashioned, I'm not putting up with it." They're the ones who are the hardest to reach. "They owe me. I didn't ask to be brought into this world! They have to take care of me till I'm eighteen." The parents have lost something there—respect, control, whatever it takes.

The problem kids are not necessarily the ones on drugs, but drugs and incorrigibility usually go hand in hand. Drugs and alcohol are easy to get, and there is a lot of peer pressure to get smashed. It's hard to convince kids not to buy into that, because it's so important in adolescence to have your friends. Kids are obviously going to rebel against their parents' values for a while. That's when parents ought to know what's going on and still remain in control. A lot of parents who are rather strict in the house, who are wonderful models, and who spend a lot of time with their kids, find out that their kids respect them.

We've been successful with the kids we've worked with. One case that comes to mind is a sixteen-year-old girl who had never gotten along with her father. Everything that happened went through her mother. The mother went away to Florida for a couple of weeks of vacation, and the girl was forced to be with the father. They had no communication whatever. So she ran. And ended up here.

He didn't understand her. He was too strict with her. He wouldn't give her any freedom. And he was nasty to her. When we called him to let him know she was here, he was so relieved . . . so relieved she was alive and well and safe! He came in for a couple of sessions, and he admitted that he did have a communication problem. That he was afraid to show her the love and affection that he had shown her when she was younger. Now she was grown up; she was developed and he didn't know what his limits were. Once that came out it was just beautiful to see! He said, "I love you—let's work it out." And she was just so happy.

I can think of another case where a kid ran because his mother was an alcoholic. The father wasn't in the house —the kid didn't even know who his father was. At first the boy refused to go home, but after we worked with him a while, he began to miss his home. He ended up wanting to get back with the mother. We hooked her into AA, and as far as we know, things have calmed down. She has had a few episodes of getting drunk, and he would end up coming back here, but these are decreasing. So I think they are working it out.

We've even been able to handle bad problems, like incest. We're really lucky in this county—we have an incest unit that is excellent. When a kid comes in with a complaint, this unit will come out and help us work with the kid and the family. One time a girl told us her father had been having relations with her for years. She was sixteen. The only reason she ran away was because he was starting with her younger sister. It was okay for her, she could handle it, but she didn't want it happening to her younger sister. We checked and indeed found that the father was forcing himself on both daughters.

We hate to remove a child from the family in such a case. We'd rather the father leave because we don't want the kid to feel punished. Or to start feeling that she shouldn't have allowed it, that it's her fault. We try to work with the whole family. The mother is usually the one who suffers most! She has sort of known all along what was going on, but ignored it because she didn't want to face it. Often the mother and father have not been having a good relationship, and he has turned to the daughter instead. There's so much hurt and pain. You really have to spend a lot of time working through that.

We have a girl here right now who is a victim of incest. Her whole family has turned against her because she told. We're looking for a place for her to live while she goes into counseling. The incest unit has a group for kids, so she's going into that. It's working well, because she realizes that incest occurs in a lot of families. She can talk about it much more easily now and realize that it's not her fault.

Then there are child abuse cases, even among teenagers. We have a kid here now who has been abused by his mother—he's thirteen—for about three years. Yesterday he was removed from the home and put here. But he doesn't want to be here. She beats him, but he wants to be with her. The mother tie is so strong, we can't persuade him to stay with us. If we try to prevent him from going, he'll probably run back to her. So it's the mother we have to work with. If the abuse keeps occurring, or if he even just feels scared to be at home, he can come back here, or call and we'll go get him. These are usually long-term cases.

Some parents respond well in such cases—there are some who almost feel relieved that you found out. "You're right, I can't control this kid. When he gets me mad, I just go off." They're relieved that someone knows, that someone is there to help them. Then there are parents who say, "Yes, I beat him. He was doing wrong. My parents did it to me, and I'll do it to him. And don't you bother me." These are the cases where the kids usually end up being permanently removed from home. First we'll try to put them with relatives who understand the problem; they will still be a little bit of family for the child. Or friends. Or we'll get a foster home. But it's hard to find a foster home for an adolescent. Especially for a white male adolescent. We just don't have them. It seems like there are more black foster parents. There is a whole different cultural attitude there. Black people are just more willing to reach out and take other kids in. White people, at least in our experience, just don't seem to be that willing.

We get about fifty percent white, forty percent black, and ten percent Hispanic. The problems seem to be the same among them all. Alcoholism in the family, child abuse, incest—about the same. When Hispanics come in it's usually because the parents have lost control of the kids to their peer groups. And most of the Hispanics we have seen have a drug problem. There is a big drug problem here.

The Hispanics are less trusting of social agencies. They feel that they can solve any problems themselves or they go to their priest and talk to him. They feel they don't need anybody's help. We haven't been able to break through that. They want their kids home. They don't want them to be in some "institution" like ours.

We've worked with Brother Michael from the church across the street several times. He's been very enlightening, explaining Spanish culture and telling us that there is not a whole lot you can do at times, because they are such a proud people. Also many Hispanic families will ship their kids off to relatives in Puerto Rico if they are having serious problems with them.

I enjoy the Hispanic kids. At first they don't trust you, but once they do, they'll tell you exactly where it's at, and what they will do and what they won't do. I appreciate that honesty.

They usually work with our Hispanic counselor. That's important to the parents. People trust someone of their own. "She understands us, she's one of us." The Hispanic counselor has been able to show a few parents what type of program this is and made them feel comfortable enough to leave their kids here for a couple of weeks. I don't know if I'd be able to do that with them—they still wouldn't trust me that much.

A couple of times we've had a situation where the grandmother is raising her granddaughter. The grandmothers are *so* strict that the girls can hardly breathe. And when they finally are allowed to date, these girls go wild! The grandmothers don't know what to do. The Hispanic fathers are also strict with their daughters. The sons can go out, but the daughters have to be careful. It all has to be done the right way. You can date only when you're seventeen, and the father has to meet the man, and you can go only here and here and here, and you have to be in at a certain time.

One of the biggest problems with everybody is peer pressure. Feeling so much that you want to be a part of something, and doing anything to be a part of that group. Whether it is having sex, drinking, doing drugs, stealing a car, anything. I think it stems from the breakdown of family life. Kids are not being supervised enough, or they're not feeling they're cared enough about. They just feel like they're worthless. They feel they can do anything they want and won't get into trouble. "My parents wouldn't care anyway if I did this, so who cares? If they lock me up, big deal." It's kind of scary. There are a lot of kids out there who feel that way.

Friends in the state department of youth services tell me that they are overwhelmed with complaints and problems about kids and that their caseload has gone way up. There are some counselors who have caseloads of thirty and forty, which is much too many. They can't do justice to the kids' problems that way. It's burning them out too.

Again it gets back to our losing that family setting, that family feeling. The family has fallen apart for some reason. It's not intentional. The father loses his job. The mother feels bored with life and wants to get out and leave the family. Both parents work. There are a lot of things that can happen—a death in the family, for example.

We've had a few kids who have experienced a recent death. Often there is a lot of anger. At the person who died and at the one who survives, because the kid is in so much pain. He's just so angry that it had to happen to him. "Why me? Why did it have to be *my* father who died? He can't do this to me. I need him!"

And sometimes the mother—if it was the father who died—is so lonely but can't talk about it to the kids. And the kids don't know how she is feeling. Or if the mother later starts to date, the kids resent the guy. The mother doesn't quite know how to explain that to the kids. I remember in one case the kid resented the mother's having a boyfriend. Finally the mother said to the boy, "You know, it's not that I don't love your father. I'll never replace him, but it's just I'm so damned lonely. I have to have somebody. And as much as I love you kids, it's just not the same kind of relationship." Once that was explained, he could understand it a bit more, although he still didn't like the man.

So many times, problems go unexpressed and resentments build and build. And then a little thing, maybe a school problem, comes up and everything goes out of whack. And you wonder what is going on. That's such a small problem. But once you get to know the kid who has come in for help, you realize there is a much deeper problem. It isn't just that he or she got suspended from school and ran.

You really have to draw it out of some kids. "How do *you* feel about it?" That's a very big question of ours. "What are you feeling now?" Or sometimes we'll say "Gee, you must be angry that that has happened to you." And then they'll finally start keying into their feelings. Or sometimes they won't. They'll just tell you it doesn't bother them. But you know by the way they're acting. They won't keep eye contact with you—they'll be so nervous that you know something is going on. They're just not willing to come out with it yet.

It's important for them to be aware of their feelings. We try to tell them that it's okay to express feelings—it's okay to be angry, it's okay sometimes to hate your mother because she abused you. You always think you have to love your mother, but it's okay to feel hate and love at the same time for her. She's your mother and you're going to love her, but you hate what she did to you. Sometimes if they understand that, a lot of kids will start coming out a little more with their feelings, and they won't feel guilty about describing them.

It's the same thing with parents. A lot of times parents will come in and say, "You know, I love my kids." And we'll say, "Of course you love your kids, but you hate them right now. How they're acting. But that doesn't mean you don't love them. You just hate living in the same house with them right now because they're un-bearable." A lot of times they'll finally say, "Yes, that's right. And it's okay for me to feel that way!"

Karen

We Get Along Better When I'm Not With Them

Seventeen-year-old Karen is staying temporarily at Harbor House. Karen is an attractive blonde, the picture of robust health. She has been through the gamut of teenage problems—running away, drugs, alcohol, trouble with the police. She speaks of her parents as the main problem, however, and her manner is aggressive, almost belligerent. She has an evident need to protest against her parents' strictness and lack of open affection for her. It is also clear that Karen is beginning to come to terms with her problems, and she may well have a better understanding of her needs than her parents have.

I've been kicked out of my house periodically since I was fourteen. My two older sisters and my older brother got kicked out too. They were into drugs in school and got into a lot of trouble. My parents didn't want to put up with it anymore. I got suspended from school for smoking pot in ninth grade, and that's when it really started.

When I was younger I started smoking cigarettes because I saw my sisters doing it. That led to bigger and better things. Which right now doesn't seem "bigger and better," but to me then it was. I thought I was cool. It was great to be accepted by all my friends who knew my sisters and brother. But then I started getting into a lot of trouble. I got caught with pot in school, my grades went down, and I started not going to school because I didn't care. In the morning before school I'd get high with my friends. Then it was "Oh, let's not go to first period, let's not go to second period," and we'd end up skipping the whole day.

Then I started drinking in school, bringing my little container with me. I started drinking a lot. I took liquor from my parents' restaurant—they own a restaurant. I had a jar every morning just to get me through the day. My father knew it was missing, but he blamed it on my sisters and brother. He didn't think it could be me. I worked with him, and I was stealing seventy to eighty dollars every other day. He knew the money was missing, too, but he just didn't want to accept the fact that it was me.

He makes a good living. He's got five children. We live in a beautiful house. My parents are lovely—I love them. Yet I didn't understand, I didn't care about anything.

You know kids nowadays. I've seen little kids, nine-year-olds, smoking cigarettes. That's how I started. If they knew all the shit that I went through! I just feel like grabbing them by the neck and telling them what I went through and that's how I started. But they're going to have to learn the hard way. They don't know what they're getting into yet. They'll say, "Oh, I'll never smoke pot, I'll never use speed, I'll never do acid, I'll never take pills"—the whole bit! But you end up doing it!

My sisters always had drugs, and I stole from my father to support my drug habit. The drugs were all easy to get. Our neighborhood was the hang. We had all the girls, and the neighborhood next to us had all the guys. This was a rich development. My parents are very wealthy. We got everything we asked for, we had everything.

I got along with my parents very well when I was younger. Then when I started getting into drugs, I didn't care about anything anymore. I didn't even care about myself. I wore the jean jackets, the bandanas around the neck, the ripped jeans, the boots, the rock T-shirts—the whole bit. My parents bought me nice clothes, but I wanted to be like everybody else.

I just wanted to be accepted by people. In school you weren't cool if you didn't smoke cigarettes and wear jean jackets. Later I came around to thinking differently, but then I robbed houses and didn't come home, and I didn't care about anything. And neither did the kids I was hanging around with because their parents didn't care about anything. My parents did care, but I figured, "Well, if these kids can do it, why can't I? Forget my parents, I'm going to do what I want to do."

See, I was fourteen, and I thought I knew everything. I thought I knew where I was going. My parents tried to stop me, but I didn't listen to them. Whatever they said for me to do, I'd just do the opposite. I felt that I had to learn myself. And I found out in the long run! I learned where my parents were coming from.

I got kicked out of my house—well, really I ran away— when I got caught drinking in school. My principal kept warning me. He said, "Next time, that's it! We're going to have to crack down and do something about it." The next day I went out to lunch and got drunk, had a couple of ludes* and got totally wasted. I smelled like a brewery when I got back to school. The principal took me into his office and called my father. He said, "We don't want her. Take her to the JINS,† do what you want with her." The principal told him, "You are her guardian. We have to turn her over to you. Then you can do what you want with her." My dad came to pick me up from school, and I ran, because I knew he was going to take me to the police station. I just ran.

I had run before, but I had ended up going home. This time I stayed at my girlfriend's house for about four weeks. Her parents didn't know I was there for two weeks, but after they caught me climbing in my friend's window they let me stay for a while. My friend's father knows my parents fairly well, and finally he went over to my house and talked to my parents. My parents said they didn't want me home unless I wanted to help myself. So next morning my friend's father brought me here to Harbor House. I stayed here a couple of weeks, and then my counselor suggested a rehabilitation center.

I was really heavily into crank.‡ I snorted it, I never shot up. I did it up my nose, and it got so bad I got sores and couldn't snort it any more. When you snort it, you get the drips down through your throat. That's the best part of doing it, because it's really potent. It gives you a sort of chill, and you get off better on it. I'd get a rolling paper that you'd roll pot up in, and I'd rip off a little piece. I'd put the line in there, and I'd roll it up and swallow it. So I was doing that really heavy. But I couldn't get it anymore, because I didn't work with my

---

* "Lude" is short for Quaalude, a mild tranquilizer. Used in low doses it produces a sense of well-being and promotes less inhibited behavior; overdoses and mixture with alcohol may cause death.

† Juveniles in need of supervision.

‡ Methamphetamine (also known as speed).

father. I had either to steal things or sell things to support my habit. I was already to the point where I needed the drips to get the best high, so I finally realized I had a problem.

I went into rehab for forty-eight days. If you were an alcoholic, you stayed twenty-eight days; if you were an alcoholic *and* a drug addict you stayed forty-eight days. I thought I was too young to be either a drug addict *or* an alcoholic.

I had a place to stay, I didn't have to go to school, and I was away from my parents. I felt rehab was fine. Two days before I was supposed to get out, I got caught for smoking a joint. It was the first time I had done anything there. A kid had come in with the pot, and he told a couple of people. We went out in the snow. We told them we were going out to build a snowman, and we went out and got high. They caught us. I swore up and down that I didn't smoke it, but I got kicked out.

My parents came and took me home. The first six months I was straight. I went to AA meetings. I didn't hang around with the same people anymore, because I figured if the drugs weren't there and the booze wasn't there I wouldn't want it. But still I wanted it. I started hanging around with a couple of AA people, younger kids, and we started drinking. I told my mom I was drinking, and she made me go to AA meetings. She would take me and sit in there. I couldn't talk in front of *her!*

The next year I got back in school. I went to what's called a pass program. It was for people that quit or got kicked out of regular school and have no place to go. The kids there got high with the teachers. It was f—— this, f—— that, every other word that came out of their mouths. They'd drink in the classroom—the whole bit. And I thought, "Oh, wow, this is great!" I figured, "What the hell! My mom thinks that I'm straight, so why let her know that I'm not?"

I started doing drugs again. I also switched schools and started going to vocational school for DE.* One night I was at a party, drinking. This kid came over and started talking to me. It was weird, because I knew his sister in AA. He knew me too. "I remember seeing you when I dropped off my sister for an AA meeting. What are you doing here drinking?" he asked. I said, "Well, what's it to you?" And he said, "Come on, let's leave." So I went with him to the drive-in, and ever since we've been going out.

It's been over a year and a half. He knew I wasn't supposed to be doing drugs. He and his family helped me a lot, because they knew what his sister was going through. He's the one who really changed my life. When we go out, we really go places. We go to the amusement park or to the movies or out to dinner. We don't just hang around on the corner any more. I love this kid, and he's the only thing I really care about now.

Last summer I didn't live at home. My father told me to get out because I came in at four thirty one morning. My boyfriend and I and a couple of people were down at the beach, and on the way home we took a wrong turn. We were in the boondocks and there was no phone. My parents always say, "If you're going to be late, call." But I couldn't call them. When I got home finally, I couldn't work the key in the front door lock. I was getting nervous. I figured I'd go out and sleep in the Cadillac. As I was opening the car door, the alarm went off. The lights in the house went on, and my dad came down. "Where were you?" I said, "We were down at the beach and got lost." He said, "Don't give me that bullshit. Do you know what time it is? It's four thirty in the morning!" Wham!

* Distributive education.

Wham! And he started punching me, hitting me. I got a black eye. I couldn't understand why he couldn't accept it that we got lost. Now, if I had made up a story, he would have believed me! The words he said to me were "The sooner you leave, the better this house will be."

Out of the five kids that my parents had, one is straight; she's fourteen. She got a scholarship and goes to private school. Every other one has done drugs or has been an addict, and every one of us got kicked out of the house. Every time I go back, the first couple of days it's fine. Then the same bullshit starts up again. They put down rules and regulations. They are very strict. I hadn't got in trouble for a year and a half, but they couldn't seem to get the idea that I was going out and doing regular things. That I *wasn't* getting drunk and coming home staggering in the front door!

So after that morning I didn't live at home all summer. I lived with a girlfriend in her apartment. It was a constant party, morning, noon, and night. People were in and out. I didn't sleep the whole time. Finally I had to go to school. I missed the first three days, but went on the fourth. I fell asleep in class. The principal came in and woke me up. He said, "You can't do this, dear." And he sent me home. "Go home and sleep and start a good day tomorrow." So I went back to the apartment. I couldn't sleep because I was speeding. There were drugs all over the place. "You want to do a line of coke?" And if somebody offers you a line, you're going to do it.* I wasn't buying my drugs anymore because people turned me on.

My boyfriend knew all about it, and he got really mad. He said to me, "It's either your drugs or me. I think you should go home. All these people do is party. I can't be

* A line of coke: powdered cocaine spread in a thin line on a smooth surface, ready to be sniffed up into the nose through a small tube.

with you all the time." He works an eight-hour day. "You can't keep on like this." I hadn't slept, I didn't eat. I was always on drugs.

I finally called my mom that day that I got sent home from school, and I asked her if I could come home and get a couple of things. She says, "Where are you? I want you to come home." So I said okay, and she came and picked me up. The first two days it was fine. It was honey this, honey that. I had already missed four days of school, but I was going to start a clean sheet and go to school, do what I had to do. I could see my boyfriend now, I could get a good night's sleep, I could eat, I didn't need the drugs.

Then on the third day my mom came home and found my boyfriend in my room. She told my father later that she walked in my room and that he was behind my door with no clothes on. That was bullshit! I was in the bathroom, and he was sitting—fully clothed—on my bed waiting for me.

She said, "What's Brian doing here?" I said, "We stopped to get something to eat for lunch, and he's going to take me to school." So I went to school, and when I came home that day, my father was already there. "Was Brian in the house today?" I said yes. "Was he in your room?" I said yes. And he started kicking the shit out of me. He said, "Go pack your things, you're going to Harbor House." So I went up and packed all my things, and he brought me here. I've been here ever since—it's several weeks now. My parents say the only way they'll let me home is if I promise I will not see my boyfriend anymore. Instead of blaming me, now they're blaming him! And he doesn't deserve it!

They came in here just a couple of weeks ago to have a conference with my counselor. My counselor asked my mom why she said that Brian had no clothes on that day, when it wasn't true. My mom said, "Oh, I didn't say that!" And my father didn't say anything!

In my family I'm always in the middle. Whenever I ask my dad, "Can I do this?" he says, "Ask your mother." And I say to Mom, "Can I go to such and such a place?" She says, "Ask your father." So I say, "Dad, Mom said to ask you." "Well," he says, "come home at ten o'clock." My mom says, "Be home at eleven o'clock." Naturally I'm going to listen to Mom and come home at eleven. I'll come in at eleven, and my dad will say, "You're an hour late." I'll say, "But Mom said . . ." "I don't care what Mom said, and I'll kick the shit out of you!" Boom! Boom! So that's how it is. He never hits me in front of my mother, because she won't go for that. But when she's not around, he kicks the shit out of me.

Now I have three places I could go. I could live with my aunt and uncle, I could go live with my boyfriend, or I could go home. The only way I can go home is to promise I'll never see my boyfriend again. I can't do that because I love the kid! I'm too young to move in with him, and I don't feel that's the right thing to do. My aunt and uncle live right down the street from my school, so it would be fine there. I called my aunt, and she said it would be fine, but she wanted to hear it from my mother that it was okay that I stayed there. Because my mom could press charges for my staying there, and my aunt could get into a lot of trouble. So I called my mom and asked her if I could stay there. She said she was hoping that I'd want to come home, and she hung up on me. My counselor called my mom today and told her it would be either living with my boyfriend or living with my aunt and uncle. Where would she rather have me? My mom said, "I'd rather have her home."

I know if I go home the same old thing is going to happen. I'll be eighteen next May, and I only have a little more time to wait. I'm sick of running. I've got to find out what I want to do with my life. For so many years I've screwed it up so bad. It's really hard in school. My brother and sisters went through this school and everybody figures, "Here comes another Halloran! She's trouble!" And they don't give me a chance. They won't let me prove myself. I've talked to my guidance counselor about it and told him I didn't think it was fair. Just because my sisters and brother were like that doesn't mean I don't want to better myself.

School itself is going pretty well. I'm in my second year of DE. It's marketing, learning about computers, cash registers, data processing, and it's really interesting. I'm taking advanced business machines, and next year, in twelfth grade, I'll be in the work program.

I still party with my friends in school sometimes on the weekends. But the only person I'm really ever with any more is my boyfriend. I don't care about those other people really. They are just old drug acquaintances. Now I guess I'm growing out of it. You get to a certain age, and you grow out of being bad. I'm just going to say no to these friends. I used to be a people pleaser, but I don't care any more. I'm number one now, and I come first. Forget all those people in school. I just have to say no when they ask if I want to get high. And that's mostly what I've been doing.

The only thing I care about right now is my boyfriend. He's the only one there for me. My parents are there to a certain point, but I can never remember them saying "Karen, I'm glad you're home. I love you." Anything like that. I can't remember the last time my parents told me they loved me.

I think they care about me, but they show it in a different way. My dad plays around with us when he shows us affection. He can't sit down and say "I love you," or sit and read a book with us, or something like that. He has no patience at all. He was an only child, and his mother and father died when he was young. He lived with his grandparents, and he had to make it on his own. He was sixteen when he took over his father's business, and he's been at it ever since. It's been a success. He makes really good money. My mom doesn't have to work —she only works part-time at a volunteer job to get out of the house. She came from a very large family, where it was warm and noisy. She has a big mouth, while my dad is usually quiet. They're total opposites.

Out of five kids, one of them is straight. My parents say it's our fault, it's not their fault. In my case I can understand that I had a lot to do with it, but my parents did too. It's not *only* my fault. But they don't see it that way.

I can't talk to my parents. They *wanted* it to be like *The Brady Bunch*, all sit down with the whole family and talk about your problems. But all I did was grow further and further away from my parents. I came and went as I pleased, I didn't talk to them. It was always Karen do this, do that. Anything my mom said to me, I always answered, "What?" She hated repeating herself, so I'd always say, "What? What?" I knew it was getting on her nerves and I loved doing it.

Our whole family has tried counseling. They spent *so* much money on counseling! When I was on probation for robbing a house for liquor when I was twelve, my probation officer suggested counseling for the family. My parents went along with it. But all we did was go in a room and bring up the past. It just makes no sense. We want to talk about the future, not the past. What we're going to do the rest of our lives if we're going to live with each other again. I'd like to see the family get together again, but it's not likely that any of the others would come home.

One sister is living in California. She left a while ago to get married and she's just had a baby. She made it, but that doesn't mean I can. Not that I want to get tied down at seventeen. I want to get a job someplace. I don't know what I want to do, but I want to do my own thing. That's where I am. I don't want *anybody* telling me what to do. I'm going to do it myself, because all my life people have told me what to do. Now I'm out on my own, and I've got to do it myself.

One trouble is, I haven't any money. I used to have a good sum of money in the bank. I had worked in a cafeteria and had money from my grandparents for college or a car. But in the rehab, they laid a lot of guilt trips on you for the stealing and lying you'd done, and I turned over my bank book to my dad. I told him I didn't want to hear it for the rest of my life that I owed him. But my boyfriend has a very good job. He just graduated from school. He works as a welder and makes about fourteen dollars an hour. He's got two cars and a motorcycle. Every other week he buys me a dozen roses.

It's not that I don't care what happens with my family, because I do care. I love my parents a lot. But we get along better when I'm not living with them. I'm going to leave in any case when I turn eighteen. My sister lives at a neighbor's house, and she's over at our house every day. She gets along with my parents so much better, because they can't tell her what to do.

That's really the trouble. Teenagers don't want to listen; they think they know it all, but they don't. My parents are older and wiser than I am, but they haven't *been through* what today's like. We're talking about a different generation.

However, if there were more parents like my parents, I don't think a lot of kids would be like they are. All my friends' parents didn't care, but my parents cared what I did. Even though I could pull the wool over their eyes. Sometimes they just didn't know what was going on, and I could get away with so many things. *Now* I can't!

That was a long time ago. You know what I've found out since? I did speed for so long that I was a different person. During that six months that I stopped doing drugs, I found out there was another person inside me. On the outside, I tried to be this big tough girl. I always liked to be the center of attraction. Yet deep down inside, I was this sweet, innocent person. It scared me, because it was like Jekyll-Hyde. The drugs made me think I was cool, I could do a lot of things that other people couldn't do. I thought I was better than anybody else. When I wasn't doing drugs anymore, I was really quiet, just sitting there. I didn't even curse! It's really weird! It's two different people. I was straight for six months, and I found out I didn't bother people, I didn't have any debts, I didn't owe anybody anything. My grades were good. I got along with people much better. I felt positive.

I've done the drugs for *so* long. I don't like that person, but I don't really know the other person. I could find out about that other person, if I just wouldn't do drugs. I could do it, but I'm afraid to find out who it really is.

I know which one my boyfriend likes the best, because he's seen them both. He says, "Why do you have to talk like that? Why do you have to do things like that? Why can't you just be nice? Be sweet. Be a lady."

It's so good here at Harbor House. It's someone to talk to, and it's great to come home from school and get a hug and "How was your day?" and not "Go clean your room and do the dishes!" It's not like my mom saying, "Did you go to school today? I'm going to call and make sure you were in school today. Did anything happen I should know about?"

They trust you here. Until you do wrong, make it that they can't trust you. And it's a lot of fun. It's not just coming home and sitting around. We have rules and regulations, too—I can understand that. You're in their home. You're a guest. And even if you don't want to talk, they'll talk to you. It wasn't like that at home.

Pretty soon I'll be eighteen, I'll be out on my own. And I want to be somebody. I'm sure everybody does. It's like a ladder you keep wanting to go up. You don't want to go down! I'm on the first rung right now. I've finally got there. And I've got to keep doing what I think is good for me. Because it's my life, and I'm going to run it like I want to.

Caroline

I Want to Bust My Brother

Caroline is seventeen and a senior in a small-town high school. She is living in an interim home after leaving her own home four months ago. Caroline's father died last summer. That was difficult enough, but she says her brother is a far greater problem for her and is the reason she ran away. Her brother, whom her mother cannot control but protects fiercely, may be mentally ill. Caroline is angry, and her manner is tough and breezy. Her optimism about the future seems unfounded; on the other hand, she is trying to get into college and away from home.

I was adopted when I was two and a half weeks old. I've never had any hangups about it. My brother was adopted, too; he's not of my blood. We've never gotten along too well. He's really insecure, with a lot of head problems. He gives me verbal, physical, and emotional abuse, and he's a *big* bruiser. When he hit a friend of mine, I said, "Okay, that's it." It was the day before my seventeenth birthday, and I moved out.

I stayed at a friend's house, but that was not too good. Things got really depressing. My friend's always had problems too. She had an alcohol problem, but she quit that with the help of a boyfriend. Her head's all screwed up now because of her parents, whom she can't stand. I'd been seeing a shrink for a while, and a social worker and the school psychologist—a lot of people. The social worker had given me her phone number and said, "If you're ever in a jam, give me a call." So I called up the social worker and went over there and stayed the night. I was really suicidal. I knew if I didn't get out of my friend's house, we'd both be little bloody messes lying on the floor, and it wouldn't be too good.

The social worker was thinking about putting me in an interim home even before I moved out, so I was sent here to this family. I've been here for four months, and I've never thought about suicide again. There's been no reason to. It's a thing of the past now.

My mother was away when I left home. She went along with my coming here because she really didn't have any other choice. Once before I took off, just for a couple of days, and she was all schizzed out. She knows why down deep, but she closes her eyes to it. She defends my brother because she doesn't really face up to the fact that he's got serious problems. Jerry never thought twice about beating me up. If I was watching a TV program with friends, and he wanted to see something else, he'd just walk up and change the channel. I'd say, "What are you doing?" and he'd simply throw me across the room. My mother would say, "Oh, don't do that!" But she's not very strong-willed.

He's four years older than I am, and he dropped out of

school. He does nothing at all. Just sits there and watches soap operas all day. He rarely goes out—maybe once a month. He stays home all the time. He gets everything he needs from my mother. She worries, but there's nothing much she can do. She's tried to kick him out, I'll give her that much, but he simply ignores her and stays in his attic room. She *has* managed to get him to go to a counselor, but he doesn't have much use for that sort of thing.

Okay, so I got fed up with all that and came here. This is great, it's terrific! There are two kids, also in high school. I came in and they accepted me, and I accepted them after a little while. I was really hesitant about coming, because I thought the mother would monitor my every move and keep a really watchful eye on me and report to my mother. Then I thought, well, I don't really have any other choice. They're just people. So I got to know them, and they're *good* people, and I get along with them all. I'd rather be here than at home. It takes the pressure off, and I like the people here better. I care for my mother, but I don't like her as a person. She's too mixed up. The people here, they're really great. They're warm and really familylike, and I missed that in the past.

I can sit down and talk—mostly with the mother. She has this habit of psychoanalyzing me and telling me all my problems. [Laughs.] I get my morning lecture, every morning. I come downstairs, and she says, "You know what I just figured out about you, Caroline?"! But if I have something really bugging me, I can talk to anybody in the family if I feel like it.

I talk to my mother when she calls, or I need the car. Or if I've got an appointment that she's arranged. It's reasonably friendly. She would rather have me back home, but if she forces me to go back, I'll just take off again, and she knows it!

I think she's trying to work all this out. The biggest

problem is my brother. At least she's got him going to a psychiatrist, and she's got me going to a psychiatrist. It's a mess, but she's trying. I don't know if there is much progress being made. We were supposed to go out to dinner, all three of us, but Jerry copped out. He just said he didn't feel like going. I said, "Mom, look, he's wimping out. He's not going to deal with it!" He's not making any effort whatsoever. I said I would sit down to dinner with him, which I haven't done in two or three years. He makes me nauseated. I just don't eat with him. But I said, "Okay, I'll go," and he backed down. In fact, he gave my mother hell for the whole idea.

This has all been going on for a long time, ever since I can remember. When my father died last summer, it just kind of compounded things. My mother didn't know how to take charge. My brother has always trod upon her, and then he started playing God. She just kissed his feet. I stood up to him, but he didn't like that, so he'd throw me around a little. He's always been that way. He's insecure, has lots of hangups. He's mentally ill.

My father and I were pretty close. He was sick for about a year before he died, so I knew it was coming. It was difficult, but I think I did okay. My brother was upset, he was *very* upset. He decided he was going to be the man of the house. That lasted two weeks, then he just cast off all responsibility, but still played God. I ended up taking on a lot of the responsibility, doing things, reminding people to do things—I was pissed off!

My mother knew it was coming, but she was really— well, still *is*—pretty knocked out by my father's death. They had a very good relationship. Very loving.

Like I said, I think I've dealt with it. I've accepted it, there's nothing more you *can* do. I always found Jerry a larger problem than my father's death. *That* was just sad.

I guess it took a normal sort of getting over, but it did take a long time.

I don't know how long I'll be here with this family. I was supposed to be here thirty days, and that was four months ago. It all depends on when we get my brother into counseling *with* me. To be able to sit in the same room and not jump at each other's throats, that's the whole idea. I'm willing to go ahead now. I'm hesitant, but willing. He's hesitant and *un*willing. Not that he ever talked about this business with me. He doesn't talk to me. We don't talk at all. Maybe an occasional grunt, that's about it. It's been that way for a long, long time.

It was easy. We didn't eat at the same table any more, so I didn't have to say anything, like "Pass the sugar." He stayed mostly in the attic. I stayed in my room and played my records or came downstairs to watch TV, have my friends over, or do whatever I was supposed to do. If he ventured downstairs, I'd go to my room or avoid him somehow. I was—am—physically afraid of him. He's so much bigger than I am, he could really whup me. He would attack me if he got upset. That's why I used to carry a knife around the house.

When I was little, he used to play games with me, just to aggravate me. He'd stand on the stairs so that he was taller than me and taunt me about never being able to catch up to him. Everything he did was to aggravate me. The most typical situation I remember was his picking me up and moving me from in front of the TV. Or he had a little habit whenever we were eating dinner together as a family, he'd dip bread into milk or the catsup and throw it at me. And he'd always get away with it! My parents never saw him because he had great timing. I'd always end up with a glob in my hair. And if I had something he wanted, forget it, it was his.

My parents came to my defense if he was hitting me.

They'd stop him. But it got to the point where he got bigger than they. They couldn't control him. He's very strong-willed. He'll think nothing of walking into somebody's room and opening up their wallet and grabbing something out of it. They couldn't even control that.

My father could do a little. He'd say, "Stop, don't do that," and my brother would stop for a little while. But Jerry would hit my mother! He never downright beat her, but he wouldn't think twice about hitting her before my father died. After my father died, he hasn't much, not unless he gets extremely angry, and then he'll slap her in the face. He probably feels he owes her *some* respect. I don't know, I can't read his mind.

Being adopted was a big hangup for him. I don't see the big deal, personally, but I guess he felt alienated. He's got no confidence. A neighbor used to say to my mother that he had definite problems because he would just slough off responsibility. And he never grew out of it.

Obviously the situation isn't going to go away in two weeks. I don't know how I'd like to see it work out. I don't want to be friends with my brother. I couldn't deal with that. Maybe get him so that he'll leave me alone and I'll leave him alone. So I won't feel revengeful every time I see him. But I don't foresee any close relationship with him ever. I think this all was his fault. I know I shouldn't blame him, but I do. My parents tried. But my mother just has no strength, and my father just did more or less what my mother told him to. You know the basic situation. I'd ask him if I could spend the night at a friend's, and he'd say, "Ask your mother." Neither of them believed in physical punishment—spanking or anything like that. I think Jerry definitely could have used it, and I'm sure I could have too.

So I don't know how long I'll be here. Now my number one priority is to get myself into college. Then I'll worry about everything else. I've applied to the John Jay School of Criminal Justice. I'll sure be happy to get away for a while and not have to worry about what's going on at home. I want to study criminal justice because I want to bust my brother. My primary interest is in walking into the house with a cop uniform on and just watching him faint! No, I'm not just hoping to get into it on the basis of revenge. [Laughs.] I think it's an interesting field.

I don't know other kids who have been in interim homes, but I do know people who have been kicked out or who have moved out. Two kids I know just picked up and moved to Florida. They're sixteen, and they're fine. No problems, it's okay with their parents. And another friend just recently got kicked out of his house—well, his parents never really wanted him in the first place. He got into a fight with his father, and his father just said to get out. I don't know what he's going to do. Right now he's living in an abandoned house that's about to be torn down. Kids are leaving home. It's happening all around, and not only kids that come from wealthy families like those around here. Though I think rich kids have a little bit of a hassle because the parents care, but they don't know how to show it because they've been brought up to respect material things too much. That's not what you need as a kid.

But I'm optimistic about the future. I don't know whether I'll be living here or living at home, whether I'll be yelling and screaming at my brother or being civil to him. I don't know what's going to happen, but I'll live through it. My mother and I are on a reasonably friendly basis and that's okay with me, but I like it here. I would like to move back, but if I can't move back, this is really a great place to be. Sometimes I feel I *should* be there, that's my home. I guess I love my mother, I don't know. I try not to think about it.

Jennifer

I Felt Nobody Cared

Jennifer is seventeen and a junior in a suburban high school. Her parents divorced when she was eleven. She seems fragile and has a slightly confused air. Two years ago she attempted suicide and grows visibly upset when talking about it. Her expression of her need to be loved and protected is nearly an appeal. She is finding some comfort from her mother and friends, but her unhappiness is deep-seated. (See the interview with the psychiatrist, Ruth, on p. 147).

My parents broke up about six years ago when I was about eleven. I was surprised, because I thought my parents got along pretty well. My mom sent me away on a trip, and when I came back she wasn't living with my father anymore. They didn't explain the reason for the breakup. My mother just told me after I came back.

They had their arguments, but I didn't think they were anything to be separated over.

It's basically my brother. He's twenty-one now, and he's an alcoholic. He used to argue with my parents a lot, and I think maybe that was the reason for the breakup. My father was not very strict, and he wouldn't discipline him, and my mother had to do it all. She was raising all three of us—I have a younger sister too—and she couldn't do it anymore. My brother used to be engaged, but he isn't anymore. He has a little daughter, and I think he's paying child support to the mother. He lives with my father.

My father lives only five miles away. I see him every other weekend. My mother and father see each other when he comes to pick us up, and they have an argument every time. They don't have any relationship otherwise.

He isn't remarried, but my mother is. My sister and I live with her and my stepfather. At first I didn't like him, but now I'm learning to accept him. In the beginning I was upset that my father didn't have anybody and my mom did. Then when I thought that my dad *did* have somebody, I wanted my parents to be back together. Now I understand that they can't be. I've accepted that.

I think my brother is rejecting the marriage. He still doesn't understand, but he's learning to like my stepfather a little better. My sister doesn't feel that bad about it. I think it affected my brother more than us girls. His alcohol problem wasn't as bad before. It was teenage drinking, but now it's really bad.

Looking back at what we've been through the last few years, I wish we *could* be back with our regular parents. I don't think I'll ever get over this wishing they were back together again. But I think they handled the breakup well, as well as they could. Nobody is perfect. It's just painful as such, but they haven't made it any worse.

I have a friend whose father was an alcoholic. Her parents got divorced about two years ago. I can talk about it with her, and that's a help. I usually feel sort of funny about it. Especially when I'm around really Christian people. When I go to church, all the kids are there with a mother and a father, and I'm not.

The family is important to me, but I have doubts about getting married and having a family. I'm afraid to get married. I'm afraid to go through what my parents went through. Sometimes I really believe that what happened to them will happen to me. But since I *know* what they went through, I can try to do things better. Other times, I think I can't. My girlfriend doesn't really talk about getting married either. She was engaged once, but she broke it off.

I discovered that when you don't have a father, you look for a boy to give you the comfort that your father should give you. When I was younger, I had a boyfriend. I thought he loved me. I was engaged to him. I told him everything, and I did everything for him that he wanted me to do. About two years ago I found out he didn't really love me. It's hard to talk about, but, well, I tried to kill myself. He came back to me then, and I was foolish enough to go back to him for a while. I was just looking for his comfort. *That* I didn't get! Now I have another boyfriend, who I think is giving me the comfort I need. I'm able to talk to him about all these things. And his family is really close. His parents have been married for twenty-five years, and it's a happy family. I feel comfort near them.

When I tried to kill myself I was confused, I didn't know what I was doing. I wanted so bad for somebody just to tell me they loved me. My boyfriend was cheating on me, he was hitting me, and all this kind of stuff. I didn't want to live. It was obviously an unsuccessful attempt, but I think it was close. My mother came home and found me throwing up all over the place. I had taken pills and alcohol. She took me to the emergency room.

I felt nobody cared. I was really desperate. It must have started when the family broke up, because I hadn't felt this way before. It certainly wasn't all my boyfriend's fault.

I still feel that way sometimes. But my mother has a lot of love for me now, because she knows what I've been through, and she knows I *need* a lot of love. I'm not really close to my father. I can tell him I love him and all that kind of thing, but I don't feel any closeness any more. I miss him, but not too much. I wouldn't get homesick for him.

A little while ago I said I really would like for them to get together again, but I know it's impossible. It will never happen. I'll have to get used to that idea.

As for the financial arrangements and so forth, my mother paid a lot. My father didn't really help support my sister and me. He had an accident and couldn't go to work. My mother said he *wouldn't* look for a job. She felt he just didn't care. So she had to do all the work, and she was angry about it.

She put down my father a lot, complained about him after the divorce. She says things like "I wish your father wouldn't let your brother have the car." She seems to worry about things that don't really concern her, especially about my brother.

She seemed to cope with financial problems *before* she was married again. Now she's complaining about money all the time. My stepfather is on social security, and he has a little side job. But we have a big house, and we've got all these electric bills. He's not making enough money to pay for this. My sister and I want clothes, and my mom is giving us money and paying the bills, and she doesn't have money for herself. So it's a difficult situation.

My father gives us girls about ten dollars or so a week, but sometimes not even that. But he's completely taking care of my brother. My father's brother lives with them, too, and he only pays my dad a little bit of money. My mother gets upset about that too!

I think things will work out with my mother and her new husband, but he might have to get another job or something. He also has a son who lives with us. He's in his early twenties and has a job. He puts his money in the bank and doesn't offer anything to my mom for groceries or anything. We *all* get upset about that sometimes. My mom tells my stepfather to talk to him about that, but I don't think he has. I think he's kind of afraid to lose his son, because he's the baby son.

Sometimes I feel like I'd like to get away. But I went to West Virginia to live with my grandmother for two years, and I got homesick. That's why I'm back here now. So I don't really think I could live away from my parents, because I miss the love they give me. So I don't think I'd move out. I just have to take it.

Christine and Amy

Christmas Is the Hardest

Christine and Amy, both seventeen, wanted to be interviewed together. They are good friends. They both started out life on farms, moved to the same town, and attended the regional high school together. They experienced similar family breakups through divorce. Neither has had an easy time growing up, but each has dealt well with her problems and has plans for the future. Both girls are obviously deeply affected by the loss of their fathers, and still show great sadness and need for support from each other and from their boyfriends' families.

CHRISTINE: My parents split up when I was four. My mother had lost a baby, and my father just kind of grew away from her. He also had a severe drinking problem. I remember sitting in the living room with my older brother and sister watching TV; my parents were out in the kitchen talking. My father called us into the kitchen individually and said, "You have five minutes to decide who you want to live with for the rest of your life, your mother or me." That was really traumatic! But my mother had always been there and my father hadn't. We all decided for my mother.

I was five when the divorce came through. I haven't seen or heard from my father in the last six years. I have no idea where he lives. He called one time and didn't even know my brother was graduating from high school. He doesn't keep in touch at all. My mother tries her hardest to make up for it, but she really can't.

She remarried in '75, and I really don't get along with my stepfather. Or my stepbrothers and sisters. There are six of them. Five of them live with their mother—well, some of them are off in college. And one of them lives with us. My own brother is in the navy, and my sister lives with us.

I think the thing that really bothers me the most is that I don't hear from my father. It's like we don't even exist any more. He remarried and has a daughter, although as far as I know he's divorced now. So he's living by himself, and I don't feel any pity for him, no sorrow, that he's all alone.

When I was ten my mother showed me the divorce papers stating the reasons for the divorce, and who was suing. My mother sued him for the divorce. My father owes my mother a lot of money. He hasn't paid the alimony, and he doesn't see us anymore. That makes me angry. Because I'm sure he does keep up with his other daughter, my half sister, who is now eight. We're his children, too, you know! In a way I'm scared to see him again. I don't know what he's like, and I'm sure he hasn't any idea what we're like anymore.

AMY: There were four boys and me, and an adopted

sister. She had been beaten very badly by her mother, so
we took her in. We were all on welfare because my father
wouldn't give us money. He was a depressed alcoholic.
He was in an institution twice. He tried to kill my mother
and me a lot of times, but my mother wouldn't walk out
and leave us kids because that would have been deser-
tion. And she couldn't take us, because that would have
been kidnapping.

So we were all living together. My mother stuck it out.
She kept us together until we got older. She figured as
soon as we reached a certain age, then each of us could
have our own choice about what we wanted to do.

When I was four we moved to E————. Those
next eight years were hard because my mother was very
ill. She had two heart attacks. With one she went into a
coma, with the other she had pneumonia. Her heart
actually stopped beating briefly, but she came back. She
experienced what's called afterlife, and she said it was
beautiful.

Finally my mother said she wanted to leave. My father
would not give her a divorce because he said he didn't
want to separate the family. [Laughs.] Which was not
true. So my mother and I left to go to Maine, and we
stayed there for seven months. The other kids stayed
with my father. Finally we came back, and a year went
by, and we . . . *they* got a divorce. Did I say "we"? It
was like my mother and I were getting away from my
father. I don't get along with my father at all.

I think the time that hurts the most is Christmas. I go
over to my father's house, and most of the family gets
together except for my brother, who is in the service. I
really didn't want to go this year. When I sit there, I feel
like a stranger. My father still lives in this house that we
all were brought up in, and it's very depressing. He lives

there with his mother, whom I don't get along with, and one of my brothers. The others have moved out now.

Christmas, I think, will be the hardest for the rest of my life. I remember when I was four years old, my best Christmas was when my mother came home from the hospital. The doctors wouldn't let her out till Christmas Eve, and then they gave her orders not to go and buy Christmas presents. So one of her friends went out and bought a whole bunch of stuff for me and my brothers. I woke up in the morning and my brothers were screaming at me. "Come on downstairs. There's a big red bow around a rocking chair, and we think it's yours!" So I ran down there and sat in the chair. Everybody was really happy that year.

In a way, the closest I came to that year was this year. It was the first Christmas in Mom's and my apartment. We had everybody over after I came back from my father's house. Everybody was so happy!

CHRISTINE: And the presents on the tree—there must have been a hundred! Just little presents, but they mean so much. I've been noticing that lately, for the first time since I met Amy, she's a lot happier. She's found someone she likes too.

AMY: Yes, I met him six months ago. He's been through a lot too. His father passed away in January. So we've remade a lot between us. And I turned around and have been able to say, well, maybe I had a rough life, but I have so much more to look forward to.

Now, my boyfriend had a real father for his whole life, loving him and everything like that, but he's just had the misfortune to lose him. So now he's got to go through a rough time. I tell him, thank God that you had a father to bring you up and make you the way you are right now. You're carrying on his traits. I never had a father—somebody to hold on to. Somebody to say, "Well, now, that was a pretty bad report card. Why don't you sit home every night for an hour and do homework." You know, there are kids going around here complaining they have it so bad—their fathers are grounding them. I'd love that discipline! My mother tries her best to do it, but she can't handle it all. To have a father to come home from work! When I was a kid, I'd see all these little girls run up to their fathers, and it was so hard for me. Because my father would come home, sit in a chair, light up a cigar, read the newspaper, and not say boo till dinner. And after dinner he'd go to sleep at six o'clock and turn all the lights out and make everybody go to sleep too. So when everybody says, "Oh, my father's so mean," I say, "I wish I *had* a father!"

CHRISTINE: I don't wish I had a father who *was* mean!

AMY: Yes, but you need somebody to talk to about everything in general. It would make everything easier in life. But there are a lot of people who have it rougher out there.

CHRISTINE: I think the closest I've ever come to having a father, besides my stepfather, was Amy's boyfriend's father. It was like losing a father all over again when he passed away.

AMY: Everybody was close to him. He was a terrific guy. It was really hard for me, especially because I used to go over there and he would say, "How'd you do in your grades?" And I'd say, "Not too good." He'd say, "Do better!" His wife still does that. She's like a mother to everybody who walks in that house. They're really terrific! So they're like my second family, and I feel really close to them. They've helped. I guess talking helps, trying to get everything out.

CHRISTINE: I remember life being hard in other ways too. Because my father didn't pay, there was a point where we were getting food from the neighbors in order to survive. Eating pancakes for dinner and not bringing lunch to school. But now my mother and my stepfather both work, and we have it a lot better. We just bought a brand new house, and things are looking up. But it will never wipe out the years that we went through before.

AMY: We were brought up on peanut butter and jelly. When we were younger, everybody would look at us and wonder, how can you do it? We had a three-bedroom house, with six kids and three adults! But we managed.

And I think my brothers are getting closer to my mother and me again. My father always told my brothers that their mother was bad, they shouldn't go near her. But my mother never criticizes my father. She always tells me to go and visit him "because he is still your father." And as much as I hate going over there, I go. Because maybe it will break the ice.

I once said to him, "Let's go out to dinner. I'll treat." And he said, "Okay, we'll go out." I took him to a nice place and treated him. But another time I asked him to go and he said, "I'm too tired right now. But it would be nice if we could bring your grandmother too." You see, he can't communicate without his mother. He's never really lived his life, because his mother always hovered over him. When we were little, my grandmother always took care of the bills. My mother could never do anything. My grandmother was the one who did the shopping and most of the housework. She just kept moving in, and my mother couldn't handle that. She even wanted to be the mother of us kids!

My father's alcohol problem is controlled now. The doctors put him on a prescription, so he hasn't really been drinking. He's laid back now, and he doesn't talk much. But surprisingly, when I took my boyfriend over, he and my brothers were very nice to him, and my father talked a little more than usual.

I feel that when I was younger—twelve, thirteen—he couldn't communicate on my level. But now that I'm starting to grow up—seventeen, eighteen—maybe he's just going to communicate better. Although he still can't believe I'm that old. I was talking to him on the phone before my birthday, and I said, "Well, I'll get my driving license soon." And he said, "You can't be that old!" I said, "Well, I am. I'm seventeen. I'm a young woman and I'm growing up."

It's hard for parents. It's hard for my mother. I'm the last. The only girl and the youngest. I know that she's going to be so lonely. I went away for a vacation to a friend's house in Arizona, and she went nuts! She really did. But she has a job doing French cooking now, so she's making out pretty well. We can go out for coffee when we want to, and sometimes we go out to dinner. Plus, I'm working, so every once in a while I help out. I redecorated the apartment this spring. She's as proud as a peacock every time anybody talks about her kids. She's really proud of us, and how we came along so well. And she knows all of us kids have a hurt because of the divorce.

My boyfriend and I have been talking about marriage. My mother says, "Just take it slow, put all the pros and cons together, and if there are more pros, then go for it. Just take it easy. Marriage is a big step, you should know how to take it in your stride. But if two people want it to work, it will work. If you can communicate, it will work out." That's how she feels. She's not totally against marriage. Everybody makes mistakes. She's really glad now she's divorced.

Most likely I'll go to college for business and managing. I like to be around people. I'd say we'll get married in two years or so. We're going to wait till we're financially set. The first year we'll save up for the wedding. The next year we'll save up for the furniture.

CHRISTINE: I want to go to community college and then go on to four-year college and become a social worker. Those are my plans. I've dealt a lot with social workers. I've talked to them about my father and I'm really intrigued with the things they do. They've given me a perspective on what I want to do with my life. The day Amy's boyfriend's father's wake took place, we sat down, just my social worker and I at the house, and we talked about all this for about two hours.

I have a lot of trouble with my mother's second marriage. I don't like my stepfather at all. And it's got to the point where I don't like my mother any more either, because she is turning out more and more like him. He's unresponsive. He picks on me for everything I do. And I notice a lot of my friends don't like him, so there's got to be something wrong with him. I mean, it can't be *all* me!

It's hard; my mom sees us growing up too. My brother is off in the navy, my sister is going to be married next fall, if her plans go right. Then there's me. I finish up high school next spring, and then I'm off to college. And I don't plan on staying at home after I'm eighteen, because I think if I stay there much longer I'm really going to ruin my relationship with my mother. I don't want to do that. And she knows it. I always say, "Is *he* going to be home? Yes? Well, then, I'm going out." That may be cruel, but she knows how I feel. So I try to get out as much as possible. There's no way around it. We just try to put up with each other.

It was very different with my father. Even if we had problems, he was very open. He would talk to us. Even when we were very little. He was only cruel when he had been drinking. He really was very kind. But then after my mother lost the baby, he lost interest in my mother. He never came home. He never talked to his kids. And when we used to go visit him later, we weren't his kids, we were visitors. That was very hard.

And it's funny. He called one time last year and found out my sister was planning on getting married. He thought she was too young. Now he comes and pops in after six years and tells my mother how to raise her kids! He said, "What are we going to do about Carrie? She's planning on getting married next year!" My mother says, "Yes, I know. There's nothing I can do." He says, "Well, you can stop her. If you don't stop her, I'll stop her." My mother says, "Whoa there, John. Listen, you weren't here for six years. Now your daughter is planning to get married and all of a sudden you call! Lay off!"

He didn't even know my brother was graduating! Now I've gone through six birthdays without hearing from him, and six Christmases. Christmas is the hardest for me, too, because I remember when I was little, my father was very handy and would make us little doll carriages, doll toys, and stuff. We had a very close Christmas when we were little.

I still have a good relationship with my mother, but I'm not as close to her as I am to my boyfriend and his sister. Marilyn and I are really close, and she introduced me to her brother. I spend a lot of time with both of them. They all want me to be in the family. They think I'm good for Lester, and he's good for me. My mother gets along with all of them too.

She's happy with Les, but she's jealous that he takes me away so much. Because one day she knows she's going to be without me, and she can't handle it. She's told me. Well, she'll have at least one more year to get used to it. Les wants me to have at least one more year out of high school to decide what I really want to do. But I know my past is past, and my future is what I have to look forward to.

Roger

A Little Fear Is
a Healthy Thing

*Roger is director of guidance in a suburban high school.
"I'm a guidance counselor for grades seven through
twelve—about thirteen hundred students. My responsibility is to care for the mental health of these kids and to
provide support services. We run a variety of programs. I
have six counselors who are employed to help carry out
those programs, help administer the needs of the students, and help deal with grades, careers, disruptive
family situations, drugs, alcohol, truancy—and the
whole shooting match of human emotions. We also have
a peer counseling group in which the kids get involved.
Whenever there's a powwow over a particular situation, I
take part in it."*

I would guess that twenty-five to thirty percent of our
kids are from homes where one parent is absent for one
reason or another—death, separation, divorce, or remar-

riage. The percentage is higher than it's ever been before; the national divorce rate is now nearly 50 percent.

The major problems that we have in school with kids from a one-parent family are behavioral. Sometimes it's depression, sometimes it's a fall-off in work, a lack of interest in school. The biggest problem comes when Mom is stuck with the kids, which I guess is most times, but it really seems critical to me when it's Mom and boys aged thirteen, fourteen, or fifteen. For some reason or other, girls at least seem to know how to play the game of school and don't mix whatever problems they're having with school. Boys tend to be much more sullen, up-front, and difficult to control. I don't know if they don't understand the situation as clearly as girls or if they just don't try as hard. Trouble often comes when the mothers are relatively young—maybe early to middle thirties—and they have a fourteen-, fifteen-year-old boy. Maybe Mom is trying to have another life, and the boy resents a boyfriend or a date.

I think that at that particular age—thirteen, fourteen, fifteen—a boy is trying to carve out his own masculinity, and if he doesn't have a father around, he can pick up all the wrong signals from other males. We've had some kids who've in effect told their mothers to go to hell. "You don't know anything about raising me. I'll do what I damn please." It really tears me up to see kids fritzing their lives like that. On the other hand, some of our best students have divorced parents. We have three National Merit Scholarship winners this year—two of them come from single-parent situations.

In the majority of cases the kids are living with the mother, and Dad in many instances is too busy, is too far away, is too removed, thinking he's not needed when there's no great crisis. And the kids feel a great deal of hostility toward him. But that's not always the case.

We're used to having new kids, who are living with Mom,
come in during the summer. But last summer we had
three boys who, after living with Mom for two years,
were now coming to live with Dad. It was summertime,
and the kids were driving Mom crazy, and we thought
that one week after school started they'd be back with
Mom. Well, that hasn't happened. They've stayed with
Dad. In one case the kid had a difficult time the first
three months of school, but his father was concerned,
really involved with the school, and now the kid is turning around. I don't think mothers have the monopoly on
being good parents.

I think it matters *when* in the child's life the parents'
breakup occurs. I think the kids whose parents divorced
when they were small—from two to ten—don't seem to
feel any tremendous impact. But twelve, thirteen, fourteen is a critical time in their development as persons
and it can be devastating to experience arguments or
lack of communication or hatred or fighting, because at
that stage they don't know if they're fish or fowl. After
that, the older they are, the better they adapt. One of
our peer counselors, a senior, who had just finished training, was told that her parents were going to get a divorce. Her reaction was, "Well, that's a shame, but life is
going to go on." I was sorry it happened, but it didn't
have the effect it might have had on her if she had been
younger.

I don't believe there are worse behavior problems
among kids of single parents than among the rest of the
school population. But we're a weird school in that we
don't have *bad* discipline problems. The kind of discipline problems we have are the kind that occur with two
parents or one parent or four parents!

Our kids are into drinking pretty much. I think it's a
big social thing. It irritates the hell out of me, but it has

nothing to do with how many parents they have. I do think, however, there is drinking because the parents condone it. Parents think it's cute that their kids can have a keg party or a cocktail party. We've seen parents throw cocktail parties before proms for twenty, thirty, or forty of their kid's friends. At our last prom, three couples were chauffeured to the prom, and they were each given a bottle of champagne by their parents to have in the limousine.

I've heard parents say, "Well, I'd rather know they're drinking at home than out on the street somewhere." I don't go along with that view. When I was in high school, I used to sneak a beer occasionally, but the fear of God and my father kept me from doing anything in excess. If kids are going to do it at home, they're going to do it out on the street, and they're going to get sloshed out of their minds when they get a chance. I think a little fear is a healthy thing!

Peer pressure is a factor, but I think the root of our kids' problems comes from the home rather than from their peers. We're living in an overpermissive age. You turn on the TV and somebody's fanny is in your face. You have to be thin, you have to have a cocktail. Where we're located, near a large apartment complex, one of the big rental agencies advertises the swinging singles life. Unfortunately, a lot of our kids are children of those swinging singles. It's not healthy.

Lindsey

We Take Care of Each Other

Lindsey is seventeen and a senior in high school. She has lived without her father since the age of two, but she has seen him frequently. She admires the way her mother took care of the family alone and has responded to a warm and trusting atmosphere by becoming outgoing, self-assured, and independent. Of all the teenagers interviewed, Lindsey seemed the least troubled by her family's breakup.

My parents got divorced when I was two. I don't really remember much when we were little except that my mother used to take me and my brother and sister to visit my dad. My mother said I always used to ask her to sleep over at his house with us. She said it used to put her in an awkward position. We visited him regularly, and we still keep in touch. We write letters. He lives in Washington now but still comes here on business and visits us when he can. I see him pretty often.

My sister was really the only one who was *that* affected by the divorce. I think she was about six and didn't really understand what was going on. My dad got married again about eight years ago. They have a daughter, who's seven. He didn't tell us in advance he was getting married. We had eaten dinner at my stepmother's house before then, I guess for him to see if we liked her or not. Then a couple of months later he got married and came back from his honeymoon and announced, "Oh, I got married." My sister really got upset. It didn't faze me. He'd always been this man whom I'd visited and called my dad. It wasn't as personal to me, because I don't remember ever living with him. It took my sister a little while to get everything worked out. Maybe if I had been a little older at the time it would have affected me more.

I didn't miss having a father around now that I look back. Every once in a while I did, I suppose. I have a friend who used to tell me that you should always have a father to live with. But I think if I lived with my dad I'd be a totally different person, and I don't think I'd want to be. I love my mother and the way she handled us all. She worked and took care of the three of us. I think she did a great job.

Now that we're going to college, it's sort of hard because my dad doesn't pay for it. My mother has to do that, and college is expensive. When my sister went to college, my mother did the best she could, but she really couldn't send much money at all. Now my brother is going to school in Washington and claims residency with my dad. My dad's giving him money, so it's different. My dad makes a lot of money and can give it. But I'm sort of surprised he does. He's loosening up, I guess. He's been a sort of a penny-pincher. When my parents got divorced, from what I understand he was to pay alimony and child support every month, but nothing else. My mother wasn't that smart about what was going to happen. She's a secretary, or an office manager, but she doesn't make that much money. Once college came, it was really hard. My dad did take out bank loans that my sister had to pay back. But now he's getting better about it: he's lending my brother money himself.

I wasn't aware of much friction between my parents. I think they argued a little when I was growing up, but it was over the phone, so I didn't hear it directly. My mom argued with my sister a lot. There was a time when my sister and my mother didn't get along at all. My sister really hated her. I remember that very well. It was in sixth or seventh grade. I think she just resented the fact that my mother was going out with other men. She was probably jealous of the attention not paid to her. But in general we have all been happy here and not upset by the situation.

The three of us kids have basically taken care of ourselves. My mother has given us responsibility always, just because that's the way she had to do it. I think we are all pretty levelheaded about what we know we have to do. And if my dad were around, I think we'd be a little more spoiled. My parents are exact opposites. My dad is very quiet, very conservative, very organized. My mother just sort of plays everything by ear. I think it would drive me crazy if I had everything organized, all planned out. Probably because she brought me up the way she did. We all take after her that way. Very open. We have a relationship with her that's like being friends—we're on a peer level—rather than she's the parent giving the rules and we have to obey them. We all live here, this is our house, and we have to make it work.

She never directly told me why she and my father got

divorced, but I think I figured it out. He was much older than she. My mom was just out of college, and she had been taught by her mother that women should get married and have babies. It seemed like getting married was something she had to do then. They were only married for a few years. I just don't think he was the right person. My mother probably needed more love and support than he could give, because he's a very closed person. It was just a mistake. When he comes here, we go out to dinner, the three of us, my dad, my mother, and I. They're good friends. It's just that I don't think they could live together. There's no rancor or anger. There might have been before, but I've never seen it, and it's never been directed at us kids.

He even took us kids across the country with him once. As a matter of fact, my stepmother was really mad at him for taking us—she wasn't with us—even though he's taken her to Europe and Israel and lots of places. That annoyed me. We're his kids, after all!

I got into the high school counseling program to help other people. I feel as though my sister helped me and my brother through a lot, and we all sort of take care of each other. Also, I think I've grown up faster than a lot of people because of having to take care of myself and having to make my own decisions. We never had curfews at our house because we knew if we stayed out late, it would hurt *us*—it wasn't going to hurt our mother! Curfews make some people rebel and stay out late—they make them mad. I'd much rather come home early, but I see it's really easy to conform to peer pressure. This summer I went to Outward Bound out west. There you can learn a lot about yourself, what you should do and what you shouldn't do, doing what *you* want and not listening to other people. So I think I can help others, and I really want to.

In the counseling program we help freshmen and new students adjust to high school and to different kinds of situations that they run into. We try to get them to know themselves and not to feel as though they have to do what everyone else does. And to feel a part of something. Maybe just to have a friend. Someone to talk to. People are lonely, and to have a friend makes a difference.

It really surprised me to hear how many people didn't get along with their parents, because I always have. When I was a freshman or sophomore, my best friend didn't get along with her parents at all. I have another friend who doesn't either, and it's hard to understand because of the relationship I have with my mother.

I'm sure half the kids in the school come from divorced parents. At least it seems like a lot do. Many of my friends' parents have gotten remarried and the kids live in two different households. I don't go up and ask them personal questions, but they just tell me they don't get along with their parents. On the other hand, they don't actually talk about divorce a lot. I have friends whose parents have recently separated and another friend whose parents got divorced a year and a half ago and his mother and father are already remarried. He's not real pleased about that. Yet those kids don't talk about it very much. If I'm feeling something, I'll go out and tell everybody about it. But I guess a lot of people keep things to themselves. So it's not a great big hot subject for kids to talk about, even in the counseling program.

Part of it is the town, I think. It's very wealthy and respectable. People are very closed here. They keep everything quiet. When people get divorced, it's not known. My mother has been divorced for a long while, but no one ever talked about it much.

Margaret

I Just Kept It All In

*Margaret is seventeen and a senior in high school. She
talked openly about her father's death, which occurred
five years ago. Margaret had clearly reflected upon the
experience and organized her thoughts about it. She
wished she had been able to deal with her feelings earlier. Her deep sorrow and sense of deprivation obviously
persist.*

My dad died of cancer when I was twelve. He had
been sick for six years. He wasn't supposed to live that
long, so we were lucky that he did. He spent the last two
months of his life in the hospital. It was of course difficult
for our family, but we knew he had cancer so his death
wasn't a surprise. I was a pretty mature twelve-year-old,
and I knew what was going on. But you can be told
somebody is going to die *tomorrow* and you won't believe it. So I never took it seriously. I took the fact that he

had cancer and that he was sick seriously, but I never really thought he was going to die.

In June—he died in August—we were in Georgia at a resort where he was having a business conference. That was the first time I ever saw him so weak. It was a big business meeting for his company, and he was unable to show up at those meetings. He was in bed. It's a horrible memory I have—it will probably always stay with me. We were staying in a two-story cottage at the resort, and my father slept downstairs because it was cooler. His lungs would fill with fluid and he had a hard time breathing—you could hear it throughout the house. That was really terrible, seeing someone so dynamic and powerful at the mercy of his illness.

We came home from there, and I left for camp. I was in camp for the last month of his life, so I wasn't there to witness what happened. I guess that month was pretty terrible. It was an anguishing time and horrible on my mother. I think she lost thirty pounds spending nights up till four in the morning at the hospital and getting up again at eight to be there again. My brother kind of making it on his own, with relatives coming to try and do some parenting. It was a hard time for them.

I guess I was still in a kind of dreaming stage. My father had wanted to come to my camp—my camp was in New York State—to pick me up. The year before, he had come to pick me up from the camp and we had spent a few days with my grandparents on the way home. This year when I went away, he said, "I'll be there, I'll pick you up and we'll drive home." Even though I knew he couldn't do that, I always sort of thought he would. Because that's the way he was: if he wanted to do something, he would do it. So I always had that little dream.

Finally I got a phone call from my mom telling me that he had died. I came home from camp, and my mom picked me up at the airport. She looked incredibly different, because she weighed so little. We got home and there were hundreds of relatives in the kitchen. I walked upstairs, and it was just weird. When I left, my father was in my parents' bedroom lying on the couch, and it was just a weird realization that he would never be there again.

I think I put everything inside then, because I didn't show very much the way I felt. My brother was more verbal, and so was my mother. It was incredibly different not having someone coming home at six o'clock. You'd go to set the table and you'd get four plates and you'd realize there were only three people. On the other hand, sometimes it wasn't that different. I think because my father spent a lot of time traveling on business. He was a hard-working person, so he wasn't home that often anyway.

Also I think it was a greater loss for me than for the family as a whole. In fact, his death in a sense enhanced family life for us. When something like that happens, you unite with the people you love. My mother and father hadn't had a very good relationship anyway, so it wasn't like we had had an especially happy home life together. But my father and I were pretty close. We were similar, and I was his favorite. He was far nicer to me than he was to my little brother. That had caused some problems with my mother and me. She started defending my little brother, since I was getting more attention from my father. After my father died, that attention was no longer there. That was probably the hardest part of it. And when it comes right down to it, she still babies my brother a little because she thought he lost out on so much.

And I resented that a lot. It was terrible. I hated it. I just ignore it now, but it was terrible in my freshman and sophomore years. I would get in trouble for everything in the world, and my brother would get away with everything. I guess that happens in every family, but my mother even admitted that she felt overprotective of my brother.

I used to have my father around to give me attention and take me for car rides and go to special places, and now I feel I've lost out on that part of my life. My brother has had that replaced by the extra loving from my mom, and I don't think I've gotten that much. Now it doesn't bother me anymore, but I used to feel it a lot. I missed my father incredibly—I still do—it's just something with me all the time. But I keep it inside. I sort of became introverted—not in the social sense—just in the family.

My brother and I go through waves. Right now I'm so busy I don't have the time to pay much attention to a thirteen-year-old. We communicate, but we have separate lives. We're close, but we're not.

I guess maybe I'm getting older, and I've learned to play games so that my mother and I don't argue or we don't try to make things unpleasant. We get along very well when we're getting along. When we don't get along, we don't get along at all. It's our personalities. I don't think we'll ever be buddies. Actually, I shouldn't say that. We get along beautifully when we *do* get along. My mother is convinced that I feel guilty about not being here when my father died. And she thinks that's the root of all my problems. *I* don't think there is any problem there. But even though I might just be having a bad day, she's sure I'm feeling guilty about my father.

She likes to get at the root of things and elaborate. Probably because she's gone through est.* We both have

* est: Erhard Seminar Training, a controversial consciousness-expanding system developed by Werner Erhard from various psychologies and business motivation techniques.

gone through est. I don't know why we did it, exactly—probably because we had friends who did. It was a great experience. It opened my eyes to many things. It made me aware of myself, and I became very pro-self instead of running my life for other people. That's the basic thing I got out of it.

So my mother and I avoid arguments. I don't mean to give you a picture that we walk around avoiding each other. We've got, I'd say, a very close family. A pretty liberal household, I think. My mother is supportive: she is open with us, and she's allowed us definitely to be ourselves. I wouldn't trade my family for anything.

It's funny, but I think that if my father was alive today, my parents would probably be divorced. In fact, my mom says that she's pretty sure that would be the fact. When my father was sick, my mom was certainly not going to walk out on him when he was in the hospital. At that point they were probably at their closest, because all his defenses were down, and she was trying to be loving. But they had talked about divorce before, she told me. And once she admitted to me—it was incredible to me—that they hadn't had any sort of sex life for years. They just didn't! I guess they weren't in love with each other and stayed married just for the kids.

If my father was alive, we'd probably be better off moneywise, whether they were divorced or not. My father died a multimillionaire. Not that we have any financial difficulties now. We live in the same house. We didn't have to make any major changes. But my father never admitted that he was dying. He knew he had cancer all along, but he never admitted it enough to make plans for us. He never signed things over to my mother and never did anything about the stocks of the company, so what we got was only a fraction of what we should have gotten. We're making it perfectly fine, but my father was negligent in not preparing the family for his death. The doctors were telling him he had three months to live, but he refused to make any plans. I suppose that's understandable. Who wants to admit that you're going to die?

His own family acted strangely at the time of his death. His mother is a devout Catholic, but in a grotesque sense. She really isn't the most wonderful person, but thinks she is. When my father was in a coma in the hospital, my grandmother would come and bring him chocolates! She would scream at my mother and tell her she was a horrible wife and that, because my mother wasn't Catholic, we were illegitimate children. She would tell my father that my mother was a bad influence and shouldn't be allowed in the room. Terrible things!

And afterwards my grandmother had a service for him in New York State. My father's family was invited to come here, but no one came. We didn't get any cards, anything. Nothing from his side of the family. And that was because of my grandmother. She told the rest of the family that after my father died we went off on vacation and hadn't had a funeral here.

It may sound like a strange, wacky thing, but it has really bothered me that I've got an entire side of my family that I used to be close to and spend a lot of time with and hardly ever see. I have cousins, and I don't see them. It is a really strange thing that they all act this way because of what my grandmother said. Upsetting, when I really think about it. It didn't bother me as much when I was younger, but now that I think about all I've lost . . . ! Mom explained to me that my father was the one who had done well and left home, et cetera. He wasn't the favorite of the family, because his brothers were jealous of him, she supposed. Just one of those family stories, I guess, but it really bothers me.

That's the time when you really need somebody to talk to. I saw a counselor, but I don't know if it made any difference—I can't even remember her name. When I was at camp, there was a counselor there who had lost her father not long before, and she was helpful. But I guess I just kept it all in.

I didn't even talk to friends about it. It's really difficult for other twelve-year-olds to deal with the death of someone's father. I got hundreds of cards and invitations to dinner and things like that. It all meant a lot, but I guess I just decided to keep it all in. I probably would have been a lot better off if I had been able to talk about it at the time, because I think it does sort of fester in me. I think at the time I thought I had dealt with it. I didn't really want to burden my mother with it along with everything else, so I didn't talk to her about it. I didn't think anybody else really understood. So I kept it all in. Now I really wish I had talked about it, because there is a lot to talk about at the time. Now it's past. To talk about it as past instead of something that just happened—it's not the same.

Randy

My Whole Family Is Women

Randy is seventeen, a senior in a large, suburban high school, and eager to talk about his family. He seems to have overcome his anxiety and distress at never having a father, though he still has a poignant fantasy of confronting him.

Randy describes the difficult times he had as a boy in a family of women, but he also underlines the values he has come to cherish. Strong now in his hard-won self-confidence, Randy plans to join the NROTC after graduation from high school.

I have two sisters, and we all have different fathers. My eldest sister's father used to be married to my mother, but unfortunately they got a divorce. My mother had several boyfriends afterward, and two of them happened to be my second eldest sister's father and my father. So we have three different fathers in the family, which isn't such a good situation.

When I was a little kid I didn't really notice it much; my mind was on playing and having fun. Back then, I just had a mother, and I thought that was all I was supposed to have. Mom took care of me and my sisters. Everybody was happy. My mother didn't say much about my father. She didn't explain why there was no one there, and I never really asked. My sisters probably knew, but they never told me, and I never talked to them about it. We were happy, just Mom and my sisters.

Not having a father really struck me during my junior high school years. All of a sudden everybody started talking about my dad this, my dad that. I just sat down one day and said, "Where's my father? What's he doing for me?" I really got a complex about it. I felt depressed and angry. Sometimes my friends would talk about their dads, and I'd just blow up at them. Jealousy, I guess. But it was tough.

Ever since I can remember, my sisters have been going off to see their dads, or their fathers would come to the house and visit them. And that, too, contributed to my jealousy. I'd think, "God, they get to see their pops. I don't get to see mine." I didn't hate them, but I sure felt they were more lucky than I was. They still see their fathers and go to visit them. But all this time, there has never been any talk about my father or any explanation for the situation.

My sisters are grown up now and married. We came out pretty well, actually, when you think about it. I think a lot of people would be pretty down under without a father, but I came through all right.

But when I first noticed it, it crushed me. It struck me all of a sudden. Other kids would say, my father's a lawyer, my dad goes overseas and does this, my father's a professor at the university. I had to lie about my father. I said he was a car dealer. It was tough. It hurt. I had to work it out. I looked at myself and said, "Hey, I'm talented, I'm attractive, I have the smarts. Some people have fathers but they don't have that, so I'll just make the best of it. If it wasn't supposed to be this way, God would have made it different. But God made it this way, so I'll just have to blossom the way I'm planted."

My whole family is women. I look back in the past, and every lady in my family never really had a man. They were married, but it didn't work out. They're all manless. My grandmother doesn't have a husband, my great-grandmother doesn't have a husband, my aunts don't have husbands. But all the women are great.

My mother is a dietician, so she's got a pretty good job and has been able to carry us along. It's been tough, though, believe me. We've all had to work.

I was always pretty worried about my mother too. My mother didn't show much emotion, but I know down deep inside she was probably hurting. I can look in her eyes every day, I can look in my grandmother's eyes every day, and you can tell it's been tough on them. But they're strong now, and they know they have to make it, so there's no sense really being down about the situation when it's not going to help.

I know my mom missed having a husband, having a partner to help out. She needs companionship. She has boyfriends, and I can see they make her happy. Once she laid down little hints to me that she was thinking about getting married. I objected. I didn't say, "No, Mom, don't get married," but I let her know I wouldn't really approve of it. I got jealous. I'd been the male figure in the family, and for somebody to invade my space—that was terrible. I was selfish, but I was very young then. I didn't cooperate at all. I'm sorry now.

I wouldn't say the same thing now. I would encourage her to get married. In fact she has one good boyfriend now, and he likes me. He's a real nice guy and he's helped me a lot. So whatever she wants to do. As long as she's happy. I want to see my mom happy.

I've seen my father before, but I haven't seen him in a long time. I don't think I will, unless I go to see him. I hope I will. I don't hate him. You might think that's funny, but I don't hate him. Hey, I love him! I'll be honest with you, my father's my father. My life has been tough, but there have been a lot of great things. A lot of great people. If it wasn't for him I wouldn't be here. I'll give him that much credit.

What does really burn me up, however, is that he has another family. Actually I have another brother and sister. I feel kind of jealous, and I feel bad for my mother. He's over in R————————, living it up with a wife and a nice family and stuff, and he leaves me with my mother. Put the burden on my mother. But I put myself where I can look at him and say, "Hey, you're not really a man. You going and leaving my mother like this, you're not really a man. And I want to be better than you." So I will. I'm going to be the man in my family that all the women deserved but never got. I'm going to represent that man!

I used to dream what it would be like to have a father. I had all these funny thoughts: it'd be great, we'd go fishing, play sports and stuff. Every day I looked at my friends and thought, they're probably having all that fun. And I'm not having it. They'd talk about what they did with their dads, and I couldn't do that. I was so jealous. Nobody talks about their mom. [Laughs.] I did though, 'cause I had to!

That's another thing, success is very important in this town. Most of the people around me are in successful families with successful fathers. I used to feel pretty inferior around those people. Wealth is important around here. Compared to those people, I'm not so wealthy. I don't live in such a nice area of town. Other people around here talk about going yachting, going skiing in Vermont, and so forth. My mom goes out and breaks her back so I can have some dinner to eat!

That's why I want to be a father. That's my goal, just to be a *good* father. How could you leave a lady anyway? I mean, if it doesn't work out, okay, but at least come back and visit the children.

When I was going through that bad time in junior high, there were so many changes in my life going on—physical, social—I just got caught up in them. I didn't know what to do and had to rely on my own self to carry through. It would have helped to have someone. I wanted a brother too. I grew up with just girls, girls, girls. I needed a male figure just to talk to, just to be with. On the other hand, being with *ladies* has helped me. Because I'm more sensitive now. I care about other people's feelings. I'm not the macho man who tells a woman what to do. I see the woman's side of things. So that's helped me become a more full person. That's why I'm good with girls now. Because I understand.

But for a while, I couldn't do anything. I didn't play basketball for a couple of years. I didn't have much confidence in myself. And I think all that could be linked to my feeling bad about not having a father, about not having anybody to support me. You know, when you're down you talk to your mom or your pop. And I didn't want to talk to my mom, because I didn't want to put any more burdens on her. So usually I'd solve my problems by myself. But maybe during this time in my life I really needed somebody to turn to. But nobody was there. My sisters were in school, and I couldn't talk to friends about that. At least not then.

I wish I hadn't held it all in, but during that time I was feeling too unsure about a lot of things. And up until that point, my life was great! I was a good athlete, pretty good student, I had good friends, both black and white. Then all of a sudden, I don't know, I just thought that I couldn't do it any more. I didn't have anybody there for me. So I got lost in myself. I wasted away. I just got lazy and didn't do anything for myself.

Anyway, I'm back on the track now. I just seem to have this ability to come through. It's natural. I don't want to go into detail about this, but I think my situation was made to be. God put me on earth for a purpose. Because nobody in my family had a father. At least a man who stays around. So I was put on the earth as a very talented young man, attractive young man, I think, very intelligent, to compensate for what I didn't have. I always had this air about me that attracted people. I could do a lot for myself without even trying. Things came easy. Things besides family life. You put aside all the financial burdens and all the family burdens, things were pretty easy for me. That really never stopped. The only thing that ever stopped me was *me*. And I did stop myself for a while, but that's over with. I've been humbled, and I know now.

Would I want to have had it some other way? No, I'm not going to say that. No, I'm happy. If that's the way it is, that's the way it is. I'm not going to say I wish it had been different.

It hasn't been easy, but I've been able to cope. Other kids have had it worse. I can remember kids coming to school, saying their parents were getting a divorce, and looking really bad, being in really bad shape. Maybe they had lived with their father and mother for ten or fifteen years, and all of a sudden there's a divorce. That can be emotionally very hard. Very depressing. But me, I never had a father to begin with, so you can't miss what you've never had.

But if I was to talk to my father now, I'd let him know something. I wouldn't be *that* friendly with him or anything. I'd just let him know that "Hey, I don't hate you or anything. I don't particularly like you for what you did, but you're still my father, and you have to live with that." I will. I'll go to see him, maybe next year when I get my navy uniform. That'll shock him. "This is ME, man!" I'll say. "I'm your son, man. Mom and I did without you, man!"

Dawn

Dad Is Still Trying
to Grow Up

Dawn is eighteen and a senior in high school. In a notably mature and reasonable way, Dawn has been able to think about her parents' breakup and the effect it has had on the family. She has learned to understand her own emotions and the behavior of her parents and brothers. Though she has often found it painful, Dawn has been able to turn her experience into a learning experience. It has helped her to feel confident about herself and the future.

We moved here from Chapel Hill when I was about six or seven. It was then my father started seeing another woman. She was a student of his. A few years later we found out that he had had another child. My mom was willing to have it work out if he promised to stop seeing the woman. And he promised that, but he didn't stop seeing her. My mom finally said she wanted a divorce.

That was hard for her, I think, because she still loved my father, but she couldn't live with him on his terms.

The divorce wasn't really that much of a surprise to me and my brothers, though we certainly didn't know everything that was going on at the time. But I remember watching TV once with my brother Lee, when all of a sudden we heard Mom and Dad screaming and yelling at each other, and Dad hit Mom. We heard her shout at him never to do that again. You knew *something* was going on! I also remember another time all of us kids were watching TV. My mom wasn't home. I had gone out to go to the bathroom, and I heard my dad on the phone in the hall. He was saying, "When can I see you again?" I was little then and I thought about it a lot, but I never said anything.

And there were other things. My father would always be out late at night, and some nights he didn't come home. I always thought in the back of my mind that he had done something, and I wondered what it was. I remember him coming home, and I was standing in the kitchen. He came on the porch, I saw him shut the door, and I thought, "He's just done something, and he's not going to tell me what it is because it's too bad for him to tell."

They told us about the divorce one September. I was twelve or thirteen. Mom was working late. We were eating dinner, and Dad told us. Mom and Dad had agreed beforehand that they were both going to tell us, so this way, Dad sort of got his foot in the door before Mom. After Mom came home we all discussed it. It was very teary and all, but you could tell right from the start it was going to be a rough divorce from the fight they had later that evening.

The whole separation part was very confusing for us kids, because we weren't sure whether they were really going to get divorced or not. It took Dad a long time to actually move out—about a year. He finally moved out into a house near the state university where he teaches. He would come to our house about two nights a week to prepare dinner when Mom worked late. Just to be with us kids. He also spent a lot of weekends here.

The divorce was very, very sticky, and they fought so much! It seemed like they were fighting because they didn't want the divorce. Then afterwards they each claimed they got the best of the divorce. Then they started playing games through us kids to sort of spy on each other. I felt that they used me as a messenger. I told them a lot of times I really didn't like it. For example, my mom would ask me, "Who is your dad seeing now?" Or "What's he doing now?" And I would get so mad! It took me a few years to say, "Hey, why don't you call him up?"

The divorce went through cycles. Sometimes they'd be on good terms, and then Dad would start coming here even more. That got confusing for Mom. She wanted her distance. She just wanted a good friendship, but Dad couldn't make the distinction. So then a few times she'd have to say to him, "You can't come anymore." But gradually he'd start coming again.

At one point he took a sabbatical and went out to Michigan. He came back because he said he missed us so much. He started staying here and began sleeping with Mom again. Only Lee and I were here then—Peter had already gone to college. We really didn't know what was going on. Then Mom had to go to the opposite extreme again and say to my father, "You can't come here at all!" Dad got really mad at her, and still to this day they're not talking to each other. It's been five years since he moved out. Sometimes Dad will call, and Mom will answer the phone. He'll say he wants to speak to one of the kids. You wouldn't think they even knew each other. It seems so hypocritical. They said they loved each other for so long!

Initially I had a lot of resentment, because I had to side with one or the other of them in order to get any affection. In our family there's a lot of love underneath, but we don't outright show it. And I was *craving* for somebody to hug me or something!

In the beginning Mom and I went through a rough time because she kept thinking that I was siding against her and that I was doing all these mean things to her. And inadvertently I *was* doing them! I didn't realize it until I talked to my aunt. I couldn't understand why Mom had so much resentment toward Dad. Then my aunt explained to me one summer that Mom quit school to have Peter, and then she had to work to keep Dad in school. When my parents got married, my grandparents didn't like it. They didn't give them any support. So Mom really gave up a lot. She wanted to stay in Chapel Hill, but Dad wanted to take the offer at this state university. So Mom left everything she had in Chapel Hill to come here, then Dad runs off with another woman! It wasn't until my aunt talked to me that I really understood what was happening.

I guess I never talked to my brothers about it. Lee (he's twenty now) was always so fatalistic about things. If the divorce was going to happen, let it happen, but he didn't want to have anything to do with it. And Peter was older. He was off to college, and he sort of cut out of it early. But I never expected it to be the way it was.

Now I think it's for the best. It's given my mom a lot of room to grow. She's doing a lot of things now that she wouldn't have been able to do. She finished up college and then started working. She has a demanding, wonderful job as a social worker, and she's working on her Ph.D., which I don't think she would have done before.

Dad is still trying to grow up. I see him fooling around all the time. I don't think that a lot of times he really knows us any more. His priorities are *not* his kids. I got in an argument with him the other night about colleges, about applying to the university, and in the middle of the conversation he said, "You know this has nothing to do with the fact that I love you." He can *say* that, but he never shows it. He'll never call and say, "Hey, do you want to go out for dinner or something?"

I'm feeling this especially now because I'm applying to college, and I need the financial aid and all. In the divorce agreement it says that Dad has to pay for as much school as it would cost to go to the state university, being that he teaches there. Lee is the only one who wants to go there. Now Dad's getting sticky about it because I didn't apply there. He won't come right out and say he's mad at me, but I think he's using it as a way to make it miserable for me. He did the same to Peter, who went to Yale. I think he uses us kids that way, and makes it miserable for us, just to get back at my mother. Like on a financial aid form which I happened to see, he wrote: "My former wife has cleaned me out." That was such a stab in the back to her!

Now I also go through phases with Mom. It's natural, living with someone, resenting someone sometimes. I resent it a lot when she asks me questions about what Dad is doing. I wish they would just be able to talk. If they could, it would be much easier for us kids. We don't know what's going on. I just wish they'd grow up!

They got married at nineteen—Mom was already pregnant with Peter. My dad's from a very Presbyterian sort of home, and that was just a no-no. Ever since, we've been black sheep. I think that was hard for him to take. We have been friendly enough with his family, but I have some other cousins clearly *the* grandchildren. When my parents got divorced, that was time for "We told you so" and "We'll just cut you out of our will."

I have talked with my mother about the divorce. In fact, we took a trip to see some colleges, and we talked specifically about it as we drove around. But I don't like sitting down with her and talking about it, because she's obviously so biased. Then it comes down to touchy issues where I don't know who is telling the truth. It's as if they're trying to get me to side with them again, and I'm trying hard to keep a level head about it. They end up stabbing each other in the back, and I don't like listening to that stuff, from either of them. Ideally, I would just love to get them together and sit down and talk with them. But I could never get those two to talk!

I thought of having all of us kids sit down with them, but *that* wouldn't work: whatever one parent says, Peter will always take the opposite position and stand up for the other parent. And Lee, who *must* have been upset about the divorce, doesn't want anything to do with it. When he was living at home, he had a lot of problems with Mom and would favor Dad. I think he is working through these problems now. He worked through the divorce. Peter was always able to step back and look at it and really be independent about it, because he didn't need my parents so much any more. He was older at the time it happened, a junior or senior in high school. So he has a very good understanding of the whole divorce. Also he's not the type to be swayed back and forth like I was. When I complain about one of them to him, he'll stand up for the other one. But when he's talking to one parent who is saying something about the other one, he won't argue. He'll say calmly, "Yeah, that's how things happen." While it just drives me crazy to have one parent say something about the other parent!

I went through a stage of anger earlier. You know, why

this family? I thought our lives would be much easier if Mom and Dad were together. Which, in some respects, they would. But they would be two unhappy people, and I think in the end that would make me more miserable.

I worked it all out on my own, mainly. I did have a good friend to talk to whose parents got divorced when she was about three. And just recently, in the last year, I'm seeing a guy whose father walked out on him when he was four, but sort of kept in touch. He wouldn't give his wife a divorce until his son was eighteen so he wouldn't have to pay child support. So my friend has gone through the same thing. He's helped me figure it out in my head, to see what's going on between the two parents, and has pulled me back from it. I'm not as caught in the middle as I was. Before, it was really hard seeing a lot of my friends here whose parents weren't divorced. You couldn't talk to them. At one point I felt like a total stranger. Not a stranger, but a different person. People were saying, "Oh, feel sorry for her, her parents are divorced." Maybe that's what I *wanted* them to feel.

But it was different once I could step back a little. I started to get a feel of where I was, and now I think I understand what happened. Their feelings for each other change constantly. I know they still have a lot of love for each other, and I think it's very sad that they can't relate on some level. They would never *say* that they aren't happy with the situation. It's too bad.

Yet I really think it's better this way. In the divorce they saw the nasty sides of each other. I don't see how they could live with each other after that. What hurts my mom most now is seeing my father stab us kids, use us kids to get back at her. Especially Peter and myself, because we won't go to the school my father wanted us to go to. My mom and Peter are paying for his education.

My father is so difficult about the money that my mom doesn't want her kids to have to go through that. So she took over. Mom can make it, but it makes her mad that her ex-husband is making twice the money she is and is so stingy.

Peter just wants to make less trouble for everyone. He's not about ready to fight a battle with anybody. He took out a lot of loans, but if Mom hadn't come through with the rest of the money, I don't know what he would have done. He wouldn't have gone up and fought with Dad.

Peter wouldn't hurt a flea. He'll just look at the good side of people and not at the bad side. Whereas me, I feel like I'm gathering ammunition to fight my parents this fall, and I *know* what's going to happen. My father won't contribute to my college expenses unless I go to State. And I don't want to go there!

I just feel that I've been screwed by him so many times. For example, when he bought his house, he said he was buying it as a place for his kids to stay. It was just a place for him to take his girlfriend! He never invited his kids. Deep down I must still have some affection for him, but it's rare when it comes out. I feel differently about my mother. I have a lot more respect for her. A *lot* more. We get on each other's nerves, which is natural, but we have good times. We both have busy schedules, but when we do have a whole day together, we'll go shopping, and stuff like that.

She understands me. I think going through so much and having to take so many different positions, to be on the defense sometimes and on the attack other times— that has all helped me a lot. And I'm seeing a man now who is much older than I am, but my mom doesn't worry about it at all because she's met him and she knows me.

So she feels I'm ready to see somebody older. I'm very independent, and I think I was forced to be independent by my parents' divorce. I don't resent it at all, because I think it is going to help me whatever may happen.

Tina

I'm Not Going to Follow in My Mother's Footsteps

Tina, eighteen, has been in prison (except for several escapes) since she was fourteen, when she was convicted of homicide by arson. The victim was her mother. Tina became a mother herself just before her trial. Her son was placed in a foster home immediately, and the state now wishes Tina to give him up for adoption. Tina has seen him once a month since birth and is not prepared to let him go. "He's already so big! He's two now. I've got a picture of him here on my desk. I've got my own little desk now—and there he sits!" Jaunty, attractive, determined, Tina has made the best of her time in prison. "I've got my GED.* I've had upholstery, clerical skills, and a little bit of electronics, and I'm a paraprofessional in homemaking. I want to go into computer repair." She hopes to start her computer training now in anticipation of parole next year. She has had a lot of time to think.

* General Educational Development. When successfully completed, the GED program offers a high school equivalency diploma.

I don't know where my father is now, but I can remember him—his face is in my head. I'll never forget him. My mother and father were not married. In fact, my mother was his kids' babysitter. I guess he'd be in his forties. My mother would have been in her late thirties. I think she was twenty-one when she had me. I don't know how she became his babysitter, but I remember her telling me about that. She never told me they weren't married. I didn't find out till a couple of years ago, when I was in the middle of some diagnostic testing before the trial. My grandmother was with me when the lady asked me if my mother and father were married. I was getting ready to say yes, because all those years I had thought so, when my grandmother just said, "No, they were never married."

That came as a shock—I was stunned! Because they were living together for a little while, and he'd be coming in and out, although I can't remember a time when he was there all the time. So now I don't know whether he got a divorce from his wife. He had a daughter and a son. I've seen pictures of the daughter, and I've met his son once. He's younger than I am, so obviously something was still going on with his wife. I ran into them together once, and my father said, "I want you to meet your brother." All these things are just beginning to come clear, because I've been thinking about my father a lot.

It's a pretty negative picture. I think of all this stuff he did to my mother. All the heartaches he gave her. I think that's why my mother turned out the way she did. Because of him. He would always abuse her. He would call up and say he'd be home at a certain time and have the food ready. She would cook something for him, and then he wouldn't come home. He'd be drunk. He would beat her. I was always seeing it. I watched him hurt my mother really badly, cut her up. I watched him slit her throat, then take the knife and cut right down her stomach. And my mother was the type of person who didn't like to go to the hospital. She hated the thought of needles. So it was hard getting her to the hospital for the stitches. And I was only little!

I don't know if her being cut had anything to do with it, but she was never able to have any more kids. For a long time I thought *I* was the cause of that—that I had done something to her insides when I was born. She would never say anything, explain why, even when I would ask her why I couldn't have a little brother or sister. So I thought *I* was the one who had done something to her insides.

But I never really had anything to do with their arguments, at least that's how I saw it later. I always feared my father, but he never actually hit *me*.

I remember a time when I was pulling his hair. I think I hated him. Although I didn't know hate from love then. He was sleeping on the couch. Something just told me to go over and sit on my father and pull his hair. He had this jet black hair. It was so thick! So I pulled his hair, and he kept saying to my mother, "Get her off me!" And I wouldn't let go.

I remember a lot of times he used to come to the house. I'd answer the door and tell him, "My mother's got a headache, and she doesn't want you here," and I'd shut the door in his face. I don't remember if I loved my mother then, but I knew she was somebody in my life. She was always there for me.

I don't know if he loved me. Sometimes I think I was an accident. All he did was take me out once in a while. It was supposed to be for my pleasure, but he always took me to these places where his friends were, where he was tending to business. He was into numbers and a lot of things like that. He would take me to a restaurant, and we'd sit at this big table and all his friends would be there. They were all men. Once I cursed at one of his friends, and I was made to apologize to him. I was seven or eight then. He's been out of my life a long time.

A couple of years ago we got this phone call that was supposed to be from my father. I answered the phone and he said, "Hello, I'm your father." My mother said, "Who is it?" and I gave her the phone. Tears started coming out of her eyes. When she hung up the phone she said it *was* my father. She told me that he said he was coming back soon. We never heard from him again after that. *If* that was him, I don't even know. I can remember the voice I heard, but I can't remember whether it was his or not. I can remember his face.

I have my mother's family name. There was a big conflict over that. He said he wanted me to have his name. She asked me if I wanted to have his name or her name, and I didn't know, so I never said. I remember another conflict over my ears being pierced. He said, "If God had wanted holes in her ears, He would have put them there Himself!"

Life at home with my mother was okay, especially in the beginning. It didn't start getting difficult between us until later. She used to drink, but it wasn't too excessive until she found out that she was going to jail. She was into bookmaking and all that sort of stuff. My father had got her into the business, and a couple of times, when she'd get busted, he'd be there to bail her out. But that last time, he bailed her out and then he left, and she never went back to work. That was good. But then she got a letter in the mail saying that she was going to court.

Then she got that phone call from him, and she just went to pieces on me.

She started drinking real heavily and having all these guys at the house. For a long time she hadn't gone with anybody. She stayed single and it was just me and her. But then things began to get really hard on me. I ran away from her once. When I came back the next day, she was on the couch with all these pills and everything, knocked out. So that was the last time I ever ran away from her. I was really scared! I never did anything like that again. And for a while things were all right between us, and then they started getting worse again.

I think the way I cared about her was wrong. I think it was more of an obligation love than a mother-daughter love. We used to be able to talk, but after the talking was done, we weren't able to *do* anything together. It was her and her drinking and her friends, and me, my drugs, and my friends. We were going our separate ways. I would bring money into the house because I was selling drugs. I would pay the bills because the welfare always went to booze and never paid the rent. We were months behind. The electric was going to get shut off, the phone, everything was just going bonkers. When I would bring money in, I always told her never to ask any questions. I think she thought I was selling my body, which was something I never did.

I could have *left!* I could have left for good and never worried about anything. But I always thought about her being in the house with nothing to eat or with no electricity.

I think I cared about her in my own way toward the end. But I don't think I cared as much as I should have or as much as I had once. I think it was more a case of having somebody to take care of. Where it should have been that she was the mother and I was the daughter, it got to be the opposite. I was the mother and she was the daughter. And it shouldn't have been like that.

This I know. She needed somebody. She was just reaching out for somebody. She wasn't a prostitute, because she wasn't getting any money for it. I had talked to my uncle about it before all of this ever happened. He told me, "Tina, your mother didn't have anybody since your father." But I just couldn't accept it then. I felt she should have still been looking after me like she had done all those years. It didn't dawn on me that she really did need somebody. She was just reaching out. She took whatever came her way. People she was introduced to through her friends—alcoholics, drug addicts, and what not. And then men started abusing her. That was her downfall. And I couldn't watch that.

I first met my boyfriend Joey playing football one day. Somebody bet me to go with him for a week. At that time I was doing anything for money except sell my body. So I took the bet, and I went with him for a week, and the week just never ended. I think that, too, was a sick kind of love. I took a lot of abuse from him. I swear I never will again, because I *saw* myself following in my mother's footsteps. So much so it's sickening! For example, me not being married and having a son and her not being married and having a daughter.

Joey knew all the pressure I was going through with my mother and the boyfriends and the drinking. I was fourteen. It was really bothering me! I told him all this because I felt I needed somebody. I couldn't talk to my mother anymore. So I confided in him.

One day we decided to go up to his house, which was a short block from my house. His brother Robert was there with his girlfriend, and his mother was there. We were all talking, and I was really upset. I was mad at my mother.

And I was straight, I wasn't high or anything, though I'd been using a lot of drugs at that time. Reefer, and I was drinking, and I was doing some acid and some pills. Cocaine. I was into drugs heavy. Anyway, Robert wanted to know what was the matter with me. I kept saying, "I don't know what I'm going to do." Because I felt like I couldn't live with my mother anymore. When I had talked to my mother about that—the first time I said straight out, "Ma, I don't think we can live together anymore"—I got smacked. I just didn't know what to do anymore.

I don't remember exactly word for word how everything went. I don't think I wanted to remember anyway. But Robert started talking about "eliminating" her or "getting her out of the way." He was trying to be a smartass. He made a noose out of some wire he was playing with and said, "All you have to do is just pull this!" And he was talking about knives and ammonia, putting it over her nose, something like that. Lighter fluid. He said if you use lighter fluid nobody would know it. There wouldn't be any evidence. I don't know if he was trying to make me more upset, but he wasn't trying to be helpful at all. He was laughing all the time he was saying these things, but he kept rubbing it in because he knew it was bothering me.

At one point I left, but Joey followed me down to the porch. I decided I was going to run away. That's what it was. We talked about that. Joey was to buy garbage bags and lighter fluid. The garbage bags were to put my clothes in; the lighter fluid was to start a fire. It was just a quick thing that we said. It wasn't planned in what room we were going to do it or anything. It was just an impulsive thing. It wasn't really premeditated.

Everything would have been fine if Joey hadn't come to the house that night! All right, he was supposed to come to the house at twelve o'clock, was supposed to bring the lighter fluid, and I was supposed to pack my clothes and run away, and that was going to be it. The place was going to go up in flames, and my mother was going to be able to get out. That was what was *supposed* to happen, my mother was *supposed* to get out. It was only supposed to scare her, to teach her a lesson. It wasn't supposed to do what it did!

Anyway, he didn't come at twelve o'clock. I had come home early and had fallen asleep with my clothes on. My mother had come and told me to take them off. She didn't like me sleeping in my clothes. So all I did was take off my jeans. She was going to put them in the wash. I remember saying, "Just leave them at the bottom of my bed," because I had five dollars in my pocket. I didn't want the five dollars to go through the wash. She kissed me good-night and said she loved me. And that was that.

At 3:36—I had a digital clock in my room—I felt a cold hand touching me, and I jumped sky high. Joey had gone to the back of the house and had climbed up a roof to my window and had come in that way. We talked for a little bit about what time it was. I said, "You know, you were supposed to come at twelve o'clock," and I think I was really trying to back out then. He said, "Well, I couldn't get out then." He went to the kitchen to the refrigerator —I remember seeing the refrigerator light—then he went to the bathroom, and then he came back in. He asked for a sheet. He had brought in the lighter fluid when he came in the window. There were matches up on my dresser. We went into the living room, and he put the sheet over the couch. Later they said the couch was pushed against my mother's bedroom door. That would mean it was intentional—that she was supposed to die. I can't remember him doing that or me doing that. We would have had to push the couch across the room—I can't remember that. But he lit up the couch, and I lit up the chair. Before that I had packed up my clothes and put them in garbage bags and had thrown them out the window. I went out the window, and I looked in the kitchen window and saw all the flames. We started running up the boulevard when he said that he was going back to see if she was going to get out. He gave me five dollars to take a cab to his brother's house across town. I left my clothes down some block, I wasn't worried about them anymore. I was shaking, hearing all those fire engines and stuff.

He arrived at his brother's house long after I did, at about seven o'clock that morning. I asked him where my mother was, I asked him what happened, and he wouldn't answer me. I kept on asking him where she was, and he just wouldn't answer me. I sensed something was wrong, but I didn't want to accept it. He finally told me she was dead, and I called him all kinds of liars. I just went crazy. I started beating on him. I thought I broke a couple of bones, but I didn't. Then I started wrecking the house trying to get to the door. I had to go through four rooms to get out, and I broke everything that seemed to get in my way.

Joey followed me. I was running, and I said I didn't believe him. He said he was going to show me and took me to a candy store, where he bought a newspaper. On the back page it said she had died. And I still didn't believe it. I had to go see for myself. I took the bus and got off at my stop and started going up to the house. Suddenly I didn't have any more energy left and couldn't do any more fighting. Joey was right behind me, and he grabbed me and wouldn't let me look at my house as we went down the block to his house. I do remember seeing the windows boarded up. He called my uncle, my father's brother, and my uncle came to pick me up. I guess Joey knew I was working with my uncle at the time. My uncle was a salesman and I was helping him on the weekend with his paperwork. We were kind of close then. Anyway, he picked me up and took me to my grandmother's house. I guess he couldn't take responsibility for me. It was my mother's mother, so I guess he figured they would take me in. I didn't want to stay there. I wanted to go with him, but I was made to stay down at my grandmother's house with all my mother's family.

You know, my mother left me in a fire one time. I was nine or ten. I don't think she did it intentionally. The place wasn't on fire when she left. She had gone out with one of her boyfriends. We didn't have any electricity and were using candles. My mother left a candle lit in case I had to go to the bathroom or something. It was a good thing I *had* to go to the bathroom, or I wouldn't be here right now telling this. I got up and the place was just all over fire. And the door was all the way over to the other side of the apartment. I couldn't get through. So I wrapped these blankets all around me and broke the window and jumped out, ran around, rang the super's bell, and told him there was a fire. They brought me to the shelter, and she was drunk when she came with her boyfriend to get me. She said, "Did you really think I was going to leave you at this shelter?" I couldn't answer her, because I felt hostility and animosity towards her then. Her boyfriend was more important than me!

But I was still too young to really understand. I didn't start putting all of this together as to why I might have done what I did until now. But I know I was really angry. Maybe it was the wrong way to get it out, but she wouldn't listen to me. I just wanted to shake her up, frighten her, make her change her life.

Okay, back to that morning. I went to live with my grandmother. We weren't close. I had never been allowed in her house, my father was never allowed in her house. They were always condemning me. Okay, now it was an open-and-shut case. I was there for a couple of weeks and then was taken to the police station for a lie detector test, because they suspected me right from the beginning. I took the test and passed. The guy shook my hand and said I was the first honest person who had walked into the place all day. Joey passed it saying he didn't do it and didn't know anything about it. That still didn't ease their minds, although they were satisfied at first. I came downstairs and I was crying. My aunt put her arms around me and said, "Thank you," because I did this all for them. They wanted to make sure it wasn't me and that I didn't know anything about it.

Then after a few days they started saying, "You did it, you know something about it!" So I ran away from them. I waited till three in the morning and sneaked out the garage door. The cops picked me up because I was out so late. The family had to come to the police station to get me. When they got me back to the house, they beat the shit out of me. They tried to break my arm. My aunt had my arm behind my back and my other aunt was slapping me—oh, it was a mess! So I ran away again, but this time I called my boyfriend and told him to come pick me up with his friend's car. And they came. I was gone for two months, living with my boyfriend in three different apartments. He was working, and I was still selling drugs. So the money was all right. Nobody knew who I was. We always lived in places where nobody knew us.

At that time he was seventeen and I was fourteen. I finally ran away from him because I was having nightmares about my mother. That's where the fighting came in. I was always blaming him and he was always blaming me. I guess his conscience couldn't take any more, and I was to the limit—I couldn't take it anymore. Things really got out of hand. It got real violent. After that day we fought all the time, physically. So I ran from him and stayed with a friend.

Joey looked for me, but he didn't find me. Later I learned that he had gone to my aunt and told her where I had last been living. Somehow they tracked me down and came and got me. I remember it was September eighteenth. I was high as a kite on reefer and beer. They brought me all the way back to my grandmother's house. Now all my family was in front of me, trying to give me coffee, telling me they were going to help me. That was the key word—help. For hours it went on and finally dumb little me said okay and confessed everything.

After they found out everything, they got kind of nasty again. After they had said they were going to help. They brought me to the police station. I didn't even make the statement—they made the statement—this is all their words in my statement. The only thing I did was to sign the paper.

I requested a lawyer, and they made up some story about the lawyer's secretary saying, "Go ahead, make the statement anyway." The lawyer was out of his office. I don't believe they even made a phone call. One of my lawyers told me during the trial that they never made a phone call. The secretary said she didn't know anything about it. So I was suckered into that all the way around.

All I did was sign the statement. It's not what I would have said if I had made my own statement. Everything they said in it was what they wanted to believe or what they believed all along; it's not really what happened.

I was sent to Youth House until November twentieth. A guard tried something with me, and I went to the authorities. They placed me in custody with my uncle. I stayed with him for a while, but then I couldn't stay with him anymore because he was scaring me by telling me I was going away for a long time, and I didn't have a chance in the world. I didn't want to hear anything like that. So I left his house. I called my boyfriend and told him to come up and get me. I told him I wanted to go back with him. That was January first.

I stayed with Joey for six months and got pregnant in January or February. Joey's mother died on June eleventh, and I went to the funeral a day or so later. That's where they got me. I was five months pregnant. I went back to the Youth House and stayed there till I had my son in October. I was called into the judge's chambers before my son was born, when I was eight months pregnant. The judge said we weren't going on with my trial until the baby was born. Finally they scheduled the court for December twenty-third. It wasn't really too much of a trial, because they went through a process of preliminary hearings and all. My lawyer told me to plea non vult.* The judge sentenced me to an indeterminate sentence, not to exceed fifteen years, in Brackley, the juvenile facility. I didn't get upset until after I walked out of the courtroom, and then I broke down. And that was it.

On January seventh I went to Brackley. By January fourteenth I had left. I didn't want to stay there. I was sent back, and in February I left again. Back again, and then I left once more in August. From August twentieth until now I've been here in the women's reformatory.

I wanted to come here. I wouldn't have run away that last time if they had just put me here like I wanted them to do in the first place. The superintendent kept telling

---

* Non vult contendere, or nolo contendere (L., "I do not wish to contend"). A plea by the defendant in a criminal prosecution that without admitting guilt subjects him or her to a judgment of conviction as in a case of a plea of guilty but does not preclude a denial of the charges in a collateral proceeding.

me, "No, you won't want to go there with adults." I knew what I was facing, I knew what I was getting myself into. Maximum security. I had known that if I ran away one more time they were going to bring me here, and they did.

I didn't like Brackley. They were just a bunch of kids that acted like babies. I never had a childhood, so I wasn't used to that. It was getting to me, I just couldn't deal with it. They had social workers there like they have here, but they wouldn't do any counseling. They'd sit in the office and talk among themselves. They had school, but I was above that level. So they couldn't do anything for me.

During the court hearings I had a public defender—in fact, four of them. And one friend: my uncle, my father's brother, the one I had stayed with. My boyfriend and I always went to court together until sentencing. He got sentenced in the morning, and I got sentenced in the afternoon. His sentence was only five years. They got him on aiding and abetting. Which I can't understand, because throughout the whole trial we both had the same charge, which was homicide by arson. I never understood that. But he had a paid lawyer. So maybe that's why, I don't know. But through the whole thing, we both had the same charge. When I found out that he had aiding and abetting, I couldn't believe it! And he's out now. I hear he's getting married, I don't know. We got back together again for a while—we wrote letters and I talked to him on the phone after he got out—but I decided it wasn't meant to be.

In fact, it's the best decision I ever made in my life. I weighed a lot of things out. I'd have to be really crazy to go ahead with that. That day at his house when we were talking of the fire, I just got disgusted. That's why I walked out of the house. But somehow it clicked later on the porch. I don't know if the fire thing stuck in my head because his brother was saying there wouldn't be any evidence, fire eliminates all evidence, but I think that's why it stuck in my head. Whether I say it was premeditated, whether the judge says it was premeditated— technically it *was* premeditated—for a split second it had to be premeditated somewhere along the line. But not to *kill* her! It was supposed to be a scare!

Anyway, Joey is out. He never comes to see me. I don't even think they'd let him up here. He was my codefendant, after all.

As for my uncle, we don't talk anymore. I wrote him a letter and told him he shouldn't feel like he was under any obligation to come see me because I was his brother's daughter. I haven't heard from him since. That's what it more or less was. He felt like he was under obligation and he did stick by me throughout the whole trial. But after I got locked up, he wasn't there anymore. It just seemed like, okay, she's tucked away in a corner, and I don't have to worry about her till she comes out. He doesn't call me and he doesn't write. I don't see my cousin, I don't see any of them.

I've been doing a lot of reading now. Kahlil Gibran—I like his writing. I've been getting a lot out of his writing as far as death and dealing with this guilt that I have. The people here—Dr. M., the psychologist, and Anne F., the social worker—tried to take me through this thing about talking about it. So I was trying to find out if I really needed to deal with it or just let it go. I read all these books—Raymond Moody, *Reflections on Life after Life*,* Elisabeth Kübler-Ross about death and dying, reflections on death. I got really depressed. So I got away from it. I

---

* New York: Bantam Books, 1977.

said, "No, I'm not doing it. This is how it's going to be. I'm not going to talk. When I'm ready to talk, I'll talk. You can't force me to talk."

It's hard for me to trust people. I found one friend in here. And one friend only. We've been friends without any arguments, without any pressure, for ten months now. And things are fine. I trust her with my life. She trusts me with hers. She's helped me a lot, because she's watched me crack up. Go in my room and put a Do Not Disturb sign on my door and just sit on my bed, looking at the ceiling, and crack up. She's watched me go through these things, and it took her to bring me out of this shell that I was in. I was letting people do anything they wanted to me, and I was going along with the flow. I can't do that any more. They wanted me to sign these papers to give up my son. Now, I wasn't going to do that! They wanted me to go into all of their programs and pour out my heart to these people I didn't even know. I couldn't do that! That's not me!

I don't feel half as much guilt as when I first walked in here. I'm not having as many nightmares. As a matter of fact, once a month is about it. Now it's getting better. And I feel that's the way it should be. I don't feel that I should live the rest of my life—it's been about four years now—dwelling on what happened. I'm sure my mother wouldn't want me to do that. What's done is done. I'm sorry. I can't right it. For me to say I'm not going to feel guilty at all would be wrong, because I am. That will always be there. But I can't right it.

I can't let it ruin my life. I have a son, and I have to think about him. There is nothing wrong with me! I've come to that conclusion, you know!

I should be going to court about my son in a couple of months. The authorities still think my parental rights should be taken from me. They say my time is too long and that it's in the best interest of the child. They say my mother's background is against me, my background is against me, that history will repeat itself. I don't see it that way. I think my son's best interest is with me. If things went wrong in your life, you try to make it better for your own kid, not *worse!*

Dr. M. is right behind me. He's doing everything he can. He's trying to help me, make phone calls for me. There's a vocational school for computer training that I've been writing to, and Dr. M. said he'd even go down to the school to check it out for me. It may be possible to start correspondence courses in advance. I should be paroled in about a year, and I want to go into computer repair. I'll have to get myself a job, get a place to live. Prepare myself to take over my son gradually from the foster family. That is, if they don't take my rights from me.

As for life in general inside here, there are times when I hate being here and there are times when I thank God I'm here, because I've learned a lot here, I'm sorry to say. But I have, and I feel I've grown up here more than I've ever grown up on the street or any place. In dealing with all kinds of women, grown women ranging in age from eighteen to sixty, they haven't shown any kind of hostility toward me being here. They weren't ever petty about why I'm here. So it's been easy for me to deal with what I had to deal with here.

I find it amazing that I had to come to jail to find myself. I never knew what I was going to do. I always thought I did, but I never did. I never knew a lot of things until I came here! Sometimes I'll go to my room and I'll think all about it. I've been doing really good. And finally, I really took a bow for myself, and I gave myself a standing ovation. And I felt a lot better. I know I've got to live my life! It's always going to be there, what's done is done, and I can't change it. All the mourning in the world isn't going to bring my mother back. So it's something that's there, but I'm not going to let it ruin my life. It took a lot for me to get where I am now, and I'm not going to let it go to waste.

Oh, there will be times, I'm sure, that I'll crack up as far as crying and thinking about it. But that's only going to be normal. And there's a lot in me that I'm not going to be able to express in words about the closeness that my mother and I once did have. And how I went through this thing where I felt she neglected me. When it was *me* who neglected *her!* As far as doing what I did. And I've been dealing with that. And now I have things worked out as best I can.

All that kind of life I had before, the drugs, the street stuff, it's gone. I mean, I'll always be a street person. If it gets so bad that I don't have a job and I don't have money to support my son, I'm going to have to go back to that. That's my only alternative. If it's not something constructive—which I know I'm going to be able to do because that's where my head is at—but if something messes up, that's the only thing I know. I guess I'll always have street in me. I'm not going to sell my body, I don't care how bad times get. I'd steal, I'd do whatever I had to do, but I'm not going to put myself that low. I'm not going to make the same mistakes as my mother. I'm full of determination. This place has given me that too. I'm really determined to get out of here and do good! Because I don't want to come back.

So I've got to go on and *live*. They say I'm going to hurt my son and do all of the stuff that was done to me. But I'm *not* going to do that! I'm *not* going to follow in my mother's footsteps. I'm *not* going to become an alcoholic! I'm going to better myself, and I'm going to make my son's life better than the one I had. I'm going to try like hell, anyway!

Ruth

It's Hard to Take the First Step

Ruth is chief of child psychiatry in a regional pediatric hospital and professor of psychiatry at a large medical school. She is married to a psychiatrist and has three sons.

I have a lot of trouble thinking of a typical teenager, because none of them is typical. But I think the kids who are able to talk about their troubles are likely not to be the youngsters who just cop out and run away or who just disappear into a grunt and a groan when family issues come up. The teenagers I've seen professionally who have had divorced parents are able to talk about it and can distance themselves and think about what's been going on.

On the other hand, probably 50 percent of the teenagers that I see are brought by someone, maybe a school guidance counselor, usually along with a parent, and most of the kids are not ready to admit that they want to see anybody at all. If you say, "What's the trouble?" they reply, "Nothing." "Gee, I understand from your folks that you've been feeling pretty miserable lately." "No." So it isn't easy to start them talking.

There are occasional teenagers who come largely of their own accord. They've gone to the family doctor and have talked some things over, and they want some help. I often get to see runaways, because they're picked up by the police and brought to the emergency room. Of course they are frightened and angry, and they don't want us to call their folks. They're hostile to anybody in authority. Their reaction to being brought by a social worker or a policeman and dumped in the emergency room and told "Now the psychiatrist will come talk to you" is "I don't want to see any shrink!" So we are on bad footing to start with.

Plus I'm older, and I think that makes it more difficult. Sometimes the residents in pediatrics or psychiatry who see them first have better rapport with them. They're closer in age, and I think that says something about what adolescents look for in a confidant. I think it's often an age-mate; it's not very likely to be someone who is older or who is in some kind of formal setting. Young people just don't come to doctors freely. Or to a hospital outpatient clinic, which is where I work.

I don't blame them for not coming, because a lot of hospital workers believe—at least in the hospital where I work—that upset teenagers who drop into an emergency room are "big trouble." And they *can* get pretty agitated when they're upset. I've had a kid throw a metal stool right through all the equipment and break the place up. An hour of quiet talking would have calmed that kid down. But that is not always possible in a busy place where physically ill people are being looked after.

So gradually the message gets across: "Don't go to that hospital; they don't want you there."

So if a kid wants help, he goes to a social worker or somebody like that. The trouble is that a social worker is largely available on a nine-to-four-thirty basis, and the troubles come on a weekend or at night, when an emergency room is the only place to get help. Or some crisis center, but there aren't very many of them.

Inevitably, some do come to us. Sometimes you can make pretty good contact. When I see a runaway, my goal is to try to work over a period of hours to get that young person back to the family and to effect some sort of reconciliation. Even if it's a short stay, to get him or her to agree to spend the weekend. Or to have a cooling-off period with a relative or friend, or in a hospital. And sometimes we're able to do that, but it's amazing the number of times we simply cannot get that kid and that parent in the same room together. By that time each of them is so hot under the collar that you're afraid you're going to lose both of them.

Let's take a runaway. I remember a thirteen-year-old runaway we looked after this fall. This young person had never known her father. Her parents had separated when she was a few months old. She had begun to stay away from school and to run away from home. She had a concerned mother, who had done a good job until the kid got to be interested in boys, when she was in junior high. She'd been a very compliant girl before, but now she began to push all the limits she could, going out with anybody and staying out late. She and her mother began to fight. The mother would have to hold her in the apartment and wrestle with her. Luckily she was quite a sturdy woman. So she was managing, but it was going from bad to worse. Finally the mother went to the school guidance counselor, who in turn took her to the local

Children's Aid Society. It provided a case worker who often mediates such cases and certainly tried very hard to work this one out. At last it was decided to introduce the father into the situation. The child had had no contact with the father, but she wanted to know who her father was. She began to maneuver father against mother. She decided maybe she'd like to go live with Dad a little while. The mother didn't want that, and they began to fight about it. And Dad wasn't really interested. He came through and made the visit, but made no commitment to spend any time with the daughter.

This went on and on until one day the kid got angry with her mother for not letting her go out with a certain boy. They had a confrontation, which brought things to a head, and she began to break up the house. She broke a big mirror, and she began to threaten, and Mom called the police. They dragged her to the emergency room. At the hospital she was quiet, and we were able to get mother and daughter together. But when we suggested she go home for the weekend, Mom said, "Listen, I'm scared. She's just broken up my house. I'm also afraid of what she might do to herself." So we took her into our psychiatric unit, hoping we could patch this up within a short time.

Well, the girl began to run away: she ran away six times from the unit. We had to call the police and fetch her out of various people's apartments. This was a girl who had not been sexually active before; now she was looking for shelter everywhere and at any price. We were really concerned. Finally we told her if she ran away again we couldn't help her anymore. So when she ran away the last time, we wouldn't take her back in. The Children's Aid people said they'd work with her, and they've made some promises to her. For example, "If you don't skip school, you can ride horses"—which she likes to do. We wouldn't make promises like that; we thought that was manipulative, but it seems to be working!

Now this kid makes a special thing of coming over to say hello to me every time she sees me in a shopping center. She seems to want to demonstrate that she's still there and okay. It's quite interesting to see that she wants contact, because she couldn't stand the sight of me before. She could avoid me without difficulty, but she seems to want to touch base. She also drops in on the ward, which is a real signal. So we're waiting it out. A social worker is seeing her, and Mom is hanging in. The girl is not doing much work in school, but she's there. She hasn't skipped school lately, because the chips are down: if she skips school, she'll be before the courts and will be shipped off to a correctional place.

So there's a girl who has gone through a rebellion and is beginning to settle down. What we really don't understand is quite why that rebellion started just when it did, except that it is a sign of adolescence.

We do see a fair amount of quite disturbed, violent behavior in adolescents. The kids have these tempers that make them throw all caution to the winds. Sometimes it's when they are on drugs or alcohol, but often it has nothing whatever to do with that.

Most adolescents have a lot of curiosity about their backgrounds. When parents divorce, kids try to maintain some kind of connection with the parent who leaves—and that is usually the dad. There is a real connection. It could be fantasy about where Dad is and what he's like and what they'd like to do with him. And it may be quite idealized.

I am working with a very bright fifteen-year-old whose parents are highly educated. Her dad has a graduate degree but never settled into any kind of useful, productive life. He runs a huge farm, has elaborate schemes, but he doesn't set up any particular house or life-style. Money is never forthcoming to pay the rent, and so on. Mom is a teacher and has to put in long hours. A few years ago she finally gave up on Dad after a lot of unsuccessful trying. They've been divorced for three or four years now, with regular, quite liberal visiting, not joint custody, but custody that allows joint decisions about most things. Yet it is not joint in many ways. Mom is having to make most of the decisions because Dad is not available to make them.

Now this youngster has decided to do what Mom couldn't. She's going to force Dad to make a success of what he does; she is going to change his life-style, come hell or high water. She's a very driven, tense-looking girl who says she's not troubled about anything. She's going to move out of Mom's house, and as soon as Dad comes up with a little money, she's going to fix up a room where he lives and look after him. It's a last-ditch effort, and she says, "I have to do it."

She'd really like it if Mom and Dad would get back together. She can't really quite understand why Mom gave up. She'll give you all kinds of intellectualized reasons—she knows that Dad wasn't providing a living and that he was off screwing around from place to place and not settling down, but she doesn't think that Mom was very understanding of Dad. And she really feels that she can make the difference. When she's telling you this, she's on the verge of tears, but she doesn't cry. And if you point out to her, "Gee, you look like you're really uptight about that, and you really are feeling sort of sad about what's happened between Mom and Dad"—well, she denies it.

In the first case of the runaway girl, the father hadn't been around at all in his daughter's life; in the second case, the father left when the daughter was eleven or twelve. From what I read and from what I've seen, it's obvious that children's reactions to a family breakup change as they grow older and are able to process things a little differently. Really young children just feel abandoned and lost and kind of scared that the other parent is going to leave. By the time they get to be ten, eleven, twelve, they're beginning to understand a little. They're torn between loyalties to each parent and are ready to take sides: they may take a strong side against a noncustodial parent. When they get to be in their teens, they're more likely to try to be fair to the last degree, which is what that second girl was trying to be—she's going to be fair, she's not going to take sides with Mom, she's going to see just exactly what Dad has to offer.

When fathers walk out, causing a family breakup for girls at age eleven, twelve, or thirteen, these girls show a lot of anger. In general, however, girls make their adjustment a little sooner than boys. Because they usually stay with their mothers, I guess it is a little easier for them to eventually identify with Mom and accept it.

I think boys have a tougher time, because that's a really hard time to lose a dad and to be in a female world. I can see why they'd have more trouble. Partly it's because Mom is making a life change and is trying to establish relations with men again, often younger men. She may be kind of flirtatious and dressing a little bit younger than she used to. I suppose it's pretty hard to be with an attractive, flirtatious mom.

When a mother is dating again, it can be difficult for a daughter too. Often she's almost competing for a man who is younger than her dad.

Some kids have had much to confront. Their lives have been filled with separations and reconciliations or different parents. Some of the youngsters I see are in their third families. For many, a family breakup means a whole change in life-style. The economics of this are pretty startling to some of them. The second girl that I mentioned came from a wealthy family with a home in a good part of town, and she went to private school. The mother had to move into smaller quarters far away from friends, and the daughter had to change schools. And there are much worse scenarios than that. Terrible things happen while the breakup is going on. In addition, the parents are not themselves while they are going through a separation or divorce. They may be quite significantly depressed for long periods of time, and they're not available to be supportive of their children. It is awfully important for a youngster to find someone who can provide support in the meantime—a grandmother, an aunt, an uncle, a friend—ideally an adult who can sort of tune in. A friend's mother and father can often do that very well.

I am working with an interesting youngster who is coping in a different way. The family hadn't got along for years and decided to break up. There were two boys, and joint custody was decided on. The parents really don't agree about anything, but they're going to have joint custody! The arrangement was that the boys would move each day: Monday with Dad, Tuesday with Mom, Wednesday with Dad, and so on. They had two sets of clothes and two sets of toys. The boy I was seeing was about eleven. Both parents were working, and he'd spend every afternoon watching the soaps.

What he actually did was develop his own soap. He had a fantasy family consisting of divorced parents having joint custody of a boy and a girl. He elaborated a whole system about how this was going to work, and he got more and more people into the act. He couldn't cope with the everyday reality one darn bit, but he could elaborate these fantasies. What will happen to him in the long run I don't know. But I think a lot of us learn how to master situations by thinking, "Well, what if . . . ?" We try out various plans and scenarios to see if some of them fit. I think it gets to a point where you have to begin to deal realistically with the situation. Adolescents are often able to do this a little bit and move away from fantasy and say, "Hey, I really can't hack this, Monday here, Tuesday there. I have to live in one place and work that out." He's beginning to do that. And he and his brother are now moving only every second week!

We also see kids in another kind of breakup situation—when a parent has died. There is less stigma, of course. If a parent dies there is often a lot of other support that bolsters the family in what is considered a normal, acceptable way. A lot of friends and family rally. And those that have churches find support there. So even if the surviving parent is depressed and unavailable, the effect is not all bad. There is evidence that kids who have suffered bereavement are exceptionally vulnerable to depression later in life, but the final word isn't in on that; there are many other factors.

I have seen kids who have gone through very difficult periods of mourning. Kids who dream or fantasize that the dead parent comes to talk with them. That's not abnormal; it's within the range of experience that one can expect at any age.

I am working with a fifteen-year-old boy whose mother died when he was about nine. At the time somebody peripheral to the family told the boy that his mother had died, and he was whisked off to a relative and remained there for years with only a tenuous connection with his father. He finally returned to live with his dad and his grandmother, and then Dad took on a new wife. Six months ago his grandmother died. The boy has been quietly angry, doing all sorts of things like soiling his underpants and hiding them throughout the house. Whatever angry things he could do, he has done. It looked like a hopeless proposition. The kid had many strikes against him. When we started to work with him, we were not too optimistic.

Well, it's turning out that he's beginning to be able to talk about his mother, and we're getting pictures of his mother and father together. He's being forced to grieve for things that he's forgotten, and he's feeling a little better, becoming a little more approachable. If this kid could make it with one person that he could trust—and we have to accept that he'll always be a little distant—he might be able to make it in society.

We've got the dad crying, too, and it's a beginning at least, but the stepmother is another story. She really is having some trouble and obviously felt better off without all of this. If the dad and the boy care for each other, it's kind of a threat to her—it's shaking the balance.

Families are complex, and of course stepfamilies are a whole other thing. Youngsters who have suffered losses are usually going to have other families. Coping with them and maintaining contacts with original parents is not easy. And things are changing at a rapid pace. Nearly 50 percent of all families are now one-parent families. It's a little hard to know what life will be like for the average teenager ten years down the road.

When you're dealing with extreme behavioral problems—behavior we don't always understand *now*—it gets even more difficult to imagine teenage life in the future. I'm talking about the kids who get drunk and go on drugs or are just generally delinquent. Mad at the world in an extreme way. I don't mean that they are disordered psychiatrically but that their behavior is difficult to understand. What we do know is that a lot of these kids have come out of disturbed family backgrounds where there has been a history of heavy alcoholism or violence or where parents haven't been around to set limits or controls. Parents who have been rejecting because of their own circumstances. Perhaps they grew up themselves not having all that much tender loving care. So it gets to be a generational thing, and some of these kids can't hack it. They're often kids who have not done very well in school. I'm not saying they're not smart enough, but they really haven't been motivated, and they've turned off to all the things that might be helpful —like sports and coaches, school and teachers, camps and counselors.

In fact, what we really don't understand well enough is what makes some kids *function,* some kids *invulnerable* to all the miseries that seem to be behind extreme behavior problems. Take kids who come from families that are really neglectful or in which, for example, the parents are depressed or insane. There may be four kids in a family like that, and three may turn out to have bad problems. Then there is the fourth kid, who really is first class, who is able to get through all that stress and be a complete, functioning kind of person. Why? All we know about those kids is that usually they've been able to find one person—it could have been one teacher or a neighbor who had a special interest in them, had them home every now and then—just somebody with whom they learned to make a good relationship that set them up. We'd like to know a lot more about those kids, but we're too busy studying the ones that don't make it. If we really understood the ones who seem to manage, maybe we would know how to help the ones who don't make it.

Of course they don't all start the same. There are some kids who are placid. The world can be falling down around them and they ignore it. And there are some kids who just are *so* sensitive to absolutely minor stresses.

I can remember one girl who wouldn't talk to me. I saw her for a whole year, and she never said one word to me. For a year I held a monologue on what I thought she might be feeling about what Mom and Dad were doing. There was a deliberate power struggle, and she wasn't going to tell me anything. And it kept on like that till she could trust me. It took a year, and it was frustrating. Now, she was pretty sick, but finally something slipped into place, and I followed her in treatment for a number of years.

It was hard. Her parents brought her to me in the beginning, and it took a while for her to understand that she could come on her own. She did finally. Then we helped her make some other adjustments. It was too upsetting for her to live with her mom and dad, so we helped them let go a little and allow her to go to a local boarding school. That helped for a while. Eventually she got back with Mom and Dad, but it was a very, very slow process. She had a family that was perhaps too close. I think they were intrusive. It was interesting that both mother and father had been identical twins. I think they had an expectation of closeness that was very special. And this youngster couldn't feel free without making a total cut.

This patient was an extreme example of how guarded kids can be. But I think it takes a long time for all of them to feel that I'm not going to welsh on them. And there are times when you *have* to welsh on them, because you know they're thinking about something life-threatening. Then you have to say you're sorry, this can't be confidential, and that makes them distrustful. The same thing happens with a guidance counselor at school who assures the youngster their talks are going to be confidential, and then the kid comes up with something pretty scary and the counselor calls in a social worker or somebody to sort it out. So the kids simply don't trust.

Then there are the kids who want to keep their interview secret. Since I have to have parental permission before I may treat a child, it's tricky, but I wouldn't turn kids away from the waiting room. I see them briefly and try to get them to tell the family and bring them in, but I wouldn't turn them away, because that's what we're here for. We ought to be available. If we put too many blocks in the way, it is counterproductive. Oftentimes the kid simply doesn't want to trouble the parent about it. Kids can be pretty protective.

Family breakups arouse strong feelings. The two that last the longest are the sadness and the great anger. The youngsters have to put them somewhere. Most kids are still being largely parented by moms, so they tend to take on the mythology that Mom may be presenting. Most of the parents I see are trying very hard not to program the kids, but it's pretty hard not to. I guess the kids have got to blame somebody, and it's easier to blame the somebody who's out of the situation. Usually that's Dad, who hasn't kept up the payments, who's out having a good time with his girlfriends, who doesn't have time for the kid on visiting day, and so forth. But it's also hard for many of the kids not to blame themselves. By adolescence most of them are over that feeling—it's the younger kids who feel guilty. But they feel angry with somebody, and some of them are angry with the parent who is still with them. Gee, what's wrong with her that she couldn't keep Dad? Did she drive him away? What's wrong with her?

There are other kinds of behavior kids can come up with. What some do when they feel lonely and abandoned by parents is get close to someone else. Or get pregnant to have something of their own, a baby, a doll, a toy all their own. Depression is a frequent forerunner of pregnancy.

Also of suicide. We see a number of suicide attempts. Very few of those are significant, but there are always some. They can be of any age group. I've seen a kid of ten take Valium. It was a small dose, but he thought it would kill him. He was the product of a messy marital disruption, and we hospitalized him because he looked so troubled. When Mom went home she found a will. It said, Please bury me with my Bible, give my teddy bear to so and so. That kid really intended to die. It was just luck that he didn't know how to do it.

It was a very unhappy family. A mother who even after separating from the husband wasn't feeling any better off, was depressed herself. I don't think this kid had anyone to provide the support he needed. There were other kids in the family, too, who were also disturbed, but they were acting out in a delinquent way whereas this kid was self-destructive. Suicide is often attempted at a point of crisis, and the crisis is often a rejection—or what the youngster sees as a rejection—by a parent or boyfriend or girlfriend or teacher. Often there is a lot of chronic unhappiness, but there is usually some sort of precipitant.

But you really have to marvel at how most of these kids do end up coping. Oh, yes, some percentage go into adulthood with feelings of depression and anger, but actually most of them turn out to be fairly productive. Patience is something you really have to have when you're working with kids, particularly with adolescents. You have to have a degree of flexibility and a sort of blind belief that things can change. There are kids who keep breaking appointments. One of my patients is a girl from a messed-up family who is promiscuous, who is on drugs, and who is doing poorly in school. Fifty percent of the time she doesn't come to appointments, but every now and then she calls. She wants to know somebody is there who is still interested, still at the other end of the line. I've had a few kids do that. Some have succeeded and some have turned to prostitution. But I don't know, if you feel that none of them is going to make it, you won't help anyone.

It's hard on parents. They often have no more patience, and it's pretty frustrating for them. It's just a disappointment, and they have a lot of self-blame. Parents feel *so* guilty that they're almost paralyzed sometimes. They need a friend on their side too.

There is help for kids and for their families. It is just a phone call away. Most places have some sort of helpline with someone who cares, someone who knows how hurt, mixed up, angry, sad a youngster can feel, someone who knows how hard it is to take the first step—and can help the youngster to take it.

Index

PAULA McGUIRE is a graduate of Oberlin College and did graduate work at the Sorbonne in Paris and the University of Münster in Germany.

She is also the coauthor, with Susan Garver, of *Coming to North America: From Mexico, Cuba, and Puerto Rico,* winner of the Carter G. Woodson award sponsored by the National Council for the Social Studies.

Ms. McGuire is an editor for an educational publishing company and lives in Princeton, New Jersey, with her husband and daughter.